Clic!

Livre de l'étudiant

Renewed Framework

Danièle Bourdais
Sue Finnie

2 Star

OXFORD
UNIVERSITY PRESS

OXFORD
UNIVERSITY PRESS

Great Clarendon Street, Oxford OX2 6DP

Oxford University Press is a department of the University of Oxford.
It furthers the University's objective of excellence in research,
scholarship, and education by publishing worldwide in

Oxford   New York

Auckland   Cape Town   Dar es Salaam   Hong Kong   Karachi
Kuala Lumpur   Madrid   Melbourne   Mexico City   Nairobi
New Delhi   Shanghai   Taipei   Toronto

With offices in

Argentina   Austria   Brazil   Chile   Czech Republic   France   Greece
Guatemala   Hungary   Italy   Japan   Poland   Portugal   Singapore
South Korea   Switzerland   Thailand   Turkey   Ukraine   Vietnam

Oxford is a registered trade mark of Oxford University Press
in the UK and in certain other countries

British Library Cataloguing in Publication Data

Data available

ISBN-13: 978 0 19 912787 0

10 9 8 7 6 5 4 3 2 1

Printed in Singapore by KHL Printing Co Pte Ltd

Paper used in the production of this book is a natural, recyclable product made
from wood grown in sustainable forests. The manufacturing process conforms
to the environmental regulations of the country of origin.

Acknowledgements
The authors would like to thank the following people for their help and advice:
Julie Green; Anna Lise Gordon; Sarah Provan; Rachel Sauvain; Marie-Thérèse
Bougard; Nicola Lester; Teresa Adams; Pat Dunn; Christine Nicholson (Waseley
Hills High School); Keisha Reid (International School and Community
College); Audrey Elliott (Castle High School); Tricia Smith (Foxford School and
Community
College); Ana Goncalves (Hall Green School); Joanne Naik (The King's CE School);
Rachel Gill (Stamford High School); Stella Pearson (Our Lady's RC High School);
Jane Baily (Wellacre Technology College); Elaine Kay (Altrincham College of
Arts); John McStocker (Oulder Hill Community School); Sarah Allen (George
Tomlinson School); Sarah Ward (Flixton Girls' High School); Joanne Roberts
(Plant Hill Arts College); Helen Dougan (The Hollins Technology College); Becky
King (Guildford County School); Alison Orr (Bishop Douglas School); Isabelle
Strode (Castle View School); Helen Garcia (St Robert of Newminster School);
Mrs J.M. Strong (Newport Free Grammar School); Barbara Thomas (Parmiters
School); Robin Spencer (Howard of Effingham School); Claire Woolley (Royston
High School); Chris Whittaker (Balby Carr Community School); Barbara Havarty
(Crofton School); Ian Brown (The Holy Trinity CE School); Alan Woodhouse
(Hamble Community Sports College); Jane Hegedus (Trinity School); Fiona
Winstone (Bartholemew School); Tim Bee (Clarendon College); Alice Coupar
(St Johns R.C. High School); Christine Buckland (The Thomas Hardie School);
Annette Hull (Honiton Community College); Susan Bayliss (Latimer Community
Arts College); Colette Thomson; Air-Edel Associates Ltd; Media Production Unit
(University of Oxford)

The publishers would like to thank the following for permission to
reproduce photographs:
p6l: Alex Segre/Alamy; p7t: ACE STOCK LIMITED/Alamy; p7b: Jeffrey Blackler/
Alamy; p12(1): Jonathan Feinstein/Shutterstock; p12(2): ariadna de raadt/
Shutterstock; p12(3): Robert Estall photo agency/Alamy; p12(4): Andre Jenny/
Alamy; p12(5): Annebicque Bernard/Corbis Sygma; p12(6): Tatiana Markow/
Corbis Sygma; p13: Galina Barskaya/Dreamstime.com; p15(1): Clara/Shutterstock
p15(2): Alvey & Towers Picture Library/Alamy; p15(3): Elena Elisseeva/
Dreamstime.com; p15(5): Flynt/Dreamstime.com; p17t: Danièle Bourdais;
p21t: Nikonaft/Shutterstock; p21b: Laurent Renault/Shutterstock; p23: Dan
Breckwoldt/Shutterstock; p24b: David Jones/Alamy; p27: Lise Gagne/I-stock;
p31l: BigStock Photo; p31r: Cardinale Stephane/Corbis; p34tl: PA Photos/
EMPICS Sport; p34tr: World History Archive/Alamy; p34b: PA Photos/Paul Smith/
EMPICS Entertainment; p37: The Print Collector/Alamy; p38: Getty Images; p41:
Andy Heyward/Dreamstime.com; p42l: Heather Prosch-Jensen/Shutterstock;
p42r: Pedro Jorge Henriques Monteiro/Shutterstock; p42b: Ingrid Balabanova
/Dreamstime.com; p43tl: PA Photos/Paul Smith/EMPICS Entertainment;
p43b: Rex Features/Everett Collection; p45: PA Photos/EMPICS Sport; p47br:
Hudyma Natallia/Shutterstock; p48l: Rick Becker-Leckrone/Shutterstock; p48r:
Jani Bryson/I-stock; p54l: Monkey Business Images/Shutterstock; p54lm:
A.Muriot/photocuisine/Corbis; p54rm: Chiya Li/Dreamstime.com; p54r: Liubov
Grigoryeva/Dreamstime.com; p54: Richard Gardette/zefa/Corbis; p55t: Stephen
Bardens/Alamy; p55b: Paul Kline/I-stock; p58l: digitalskillet/I-stock; p58r:
Hutchison Picture Library; p60t: Monkey Business Images/Shutterstock; p60r:
Andrea Skjold/Dreamstime.com; p60b: Shaun Lowe/I-stock; p61t: Ferenc Ungor/
Dreamstime.com; p63: Kristian Sekulic/Shutterstock; p66(1): Stephen Strathdee/
Shutterstock; p66(2): Lepas/Dreamstime.com; p66(3): Mike Flippo/Shutterstock;
p66(4): Elnur/Shutterstock; p66(6): Luminis/Shutterstock; p66(7): Evaletova/
Dreamstime.com; p66(8): Oleksandr Kalyna/Dreamstime.com; p66(9): Norman
Pogson/Dreamstime.com; p66(10): Commonrepublic/Dreamstime.com; p66(11):
Larisa Lofitskaya/Shutterstock; p66(12): ene/Shutterstock; p67(1): Matt Antonino/
Shutterstock; p67(2): Kameel4u/Shutterstock; p67(3): Photodisc/Getty Images;
p69: Kathy Hancock/Alamy; p70(b): Color Day Production/Getty Images; p70(d):
John Lund/Marc Romanelli/Getty Images; p71: Yuri Arcurs/Shutterstock;
p72(1): Clara/Shutterstock; p72(2): Mark Boulton/Alamy; p72(3): Moviestore
Collection/Warner Bros POK002; p72(4): Nina Shannon/I-stock; p72(6): Stefano
Bianchetti/Corbis; p72(a): Gravicapa/Shutterstock; p72(b): Monkey Business
Images/Shutterstock; p72(d): Nick Stubbs/Dreamstime.com; p72(e): David Davis/
Dreamstime.com; p72(f): Mark Hryciw/Dreamstime.com; p73t: Owen Franken/
Corbis; p73:l: Ramsey Houck/I-stock; p73:ml: Michael Ledray/Shutterstock;
p73mr: Corbis/Hasbro/Handout/Reuters; p73r: Getty Images; p73b: NoirVision/
Shutterstock; p78l: imagebroker/Alamy; p78r: Directphoto.org/Alamy; p79(a):
Robert Nystrom/BigStock Photo; p79(b): Hasan Serdar Çelik/Dreamstime; p79(c):
Corbis/Nancy Kaszerman/ZUMA; p79(e): Johanna Goodyear/Dreamstime.com;
p79(f): Andrew Woodley/Alamy; p81: Getty Images/WireImage; p82: PA Photos/
Mark Baker/AP; p83: Bembaron Jeremy/Corbis; p84: Getty Images/Bongarts;
p85(4): Liljaphoto/Dreamstime.com; p85(5): Oleg Filipchuk/Dreamstime.com;
p85(6): Rod Ferris/Shutterstock; p85(7): Jack Dagley Photography/Shutterstock;
p85(8): Csaba Peterdi/Shutterstock; p85(9): Grosremy/Dreamstime.com; p86(a):
Cenorman/Dreamstime; p86(b): Wojciech Gajda/Dreamstime; p86(c): Steven
Pepple/Dreamstime; p86(d): Jacom Stephens/I-stock; p88: ARTPOSE Adam
Borkowski/Shutterstock; p89r: Ekaterina Monakhova/I-stock; p90: PA Photos/
Charles Krupa/AP; p91l: PA Photos/Mark Baker/AP; p91m: PA Photos/Gouhier
Nicolas/ABACA; p91r: Rex Features/Sipa Press; p92: Hixson/Dreamstime.com;
p95: Marc Pagani Photography/Shutterstock; p96t: Gelpi/Shutterstock; p96m:
Larry St. Pierre/Shutterstock; p96b: Ling Xia/Dreamstime.com; p97t: Nick Schlax/
I-stock; p97b: Slonov/Dreamstime; p99: Ryan McVay/Getty Images; p100: Olga
Besnard/Shutterstock; p101: Idealink Photography/Alamy; p102(b): Jules Studio/
Shutterstock; p102(c): Miodrag Gajic/Shutterstock; p102(d): Raycan/Dreamstime.
com; p102(e): Darren Baker/Dreamstime.com; p102(f): lukaszfus/Shutterstock;
p102(g): picturesbyrob/Alamy; p102(h): Damir Karan/Shutterstock; p103t: Big
Stock; p103b: Oleg Prikhodko/I-stock; p104tl: GurganusImages/Shutterstock;
p104tr: Photoeuphoria/Dreamstime.com; p104bl: Ejwhite/Dreamstime.
com; p104br: Suzanne Tucker/Shutterstock; p105tl: Jkitan/Dreamstime.com;
p105tr: vario images GmbH & Co.KG/Alamy; p105ml: Adam Korzekwa/I-stock;
p105m: Vera Bogaerts/Shutterstock; p105mr: Andrey Armyagov/Shutterstock;
p105bl: Glenn Harper/Alamy; p105bm: Andrey Armyagov/Shutterstock;
p105br: Dmitry Sladkov/Dreamstime.com; p105b: Susan Gottberg/Dreamstime.
com; p107l: ARTPOSE Adam Borkowski/Shutterstock; p108: Elena Elisseeva/
Shutterstock; p114l: Monkey Business Images/Shutterstock; p114r: Libby Welch/
Alamy; p117l: Dmitriy Shironosov/Shutterstock; p117(a): Robert Fried/Alamy;
p117(b): PA Photos/Marco Garcia/AP; p117(c): Dmitriy Shironosov/Dreamstime.
com; p117(e): David Jones/Alamy; p120(1): Rex Features/Everett Collection;
p120(2): Rex Features/c.Pathe/Everett; p120(3): Rex Features/Everett Collection;
p120(4): Cinebook Ltd; p121: Moviestore Collection; p122tr: Tracy Whiteside/
Shutterstock; p122bl: Heather Prosch-Jensen/Shutterstock; p122br: Joselito
Briones/I-stock; p123t: Rex Features; p123b: www.cite-espace.com p125t: PA
Photos/Jean Bibard/Panoramic; p125bl: Getty Images/AFP; p125br: Rex Features/
Sipa Press; p126: Jose Gil/Dreamstime.com; p127t: Hamiza Bakirci/Dreamstime.
com; p127m: Elena Elisseeva/Dreamstime.com; p127b: Julia Pivovarova/I-stock;
p128: AVAVA/Shutterstock.

All other photographs provided by Oxford University Press.

Illustrations by:
Adrian Barclay, Mark Draisey, Maya Gavin, John Hallett, Gemma Hastilow,
Mike Lacey, Nigel Paige, Sean Parkes, Mike Phillips, Olivier Prime, Pulsar,
Simon Tegg, Theresa Tibbetts, Frederique Vayssieres, Laszlo Veres

Bienvenue à

Welcome to *Clic!* where you will

- learn to speak and understand French
- find out interesting facts about France, French-speaking countries and the people who live and work there
- develop strategies to help you with your learning.

Meet Joe, Max and Nina. Join them as they visit Paris (in this book and on the *Clic!* video).

Meet other young French people in the *Clic!* podcasts.

Joe

Max

Nina

Symbols and headings you will find in the book: what do they mean?
Look through the book and find an example of each one.

 Watch the video

 Be careful!

 A quick revision test to check what you have learnt

 A listening activity

 A speaking activity

(B → A) Now swap roles with your partner (in a speaking activity)

 A video activity

 A reading activity

 A writing activity

 A grammar activity

Stratégies A skills activity

Défi! A challenge

 Important words or phrases

Labo-langue	Grammar explanations and practice, learning strategies and pronunciation practice
Blog-notes	Activities linked to video blog (in preparation for the checklist in the *En solo* Workbook)
clic.fr	Information about France
Vocabulaire	Unit vocabulary list
On chante!	A song
Lecture	Reading pages
En plus	Reinforcement and extension activities
Grammaire	Grammar reference
Glossaire	Bilingual glossary

Table des matières

Départ

● Personal details, greetings

In Clic 2, there is a new video at the start of each unit. It takes you to Paris where you will meet young French people and find out what it is like to be a teenager in the French capital!

Voici Joe Samson. Il a 15 ans. Il est anglais et il habite à Londres. Aujourd'hui, Joe va à Paris chez son correspondant.

Londres

Voici Max Lantier, le correspondant de Joe. Il a 16 ans. Il est français et il habite à Paris.

Joe voyage en Eurostar. Le voyage Londres–Paris, c'est 2 h 15 à plus de 300 kilomètres à l'heure!

Paris

Et voici Nina Batesti. C'est une copine de Max. Elle a 15 ans, elle est française et elle aussi habite à Paris.

1 Regarde le clip. Observe et fais le quiz!
Watch the clip. How observant are you?
Choose 'a' or 'b'.

1 Joe a…
  a un billet d'Eurostar.
  b un billet et un passeport.

2 L'Eurostar est…
  a blanc et rouge.   **b** blanc et orange.

3 Le train pour Paris est à…
  a 11 h 59.   **b** 12 h 30..

4 Le train part du quai*…
  a numéro 8. **b** numéro 9.   *platform

5 Quand Max voit Joe, il dit…
  a Salut! **b** Bienvenue!

6 La gare à Paris s'appelle…
  a la Gare du Nord. **b** la Gare du Port.

2b Relie.
Match the French to the English.

How are you?
Have a good trip!
Let's go!
Did you have a good trip?
I'm fine. And you?

a Bon voyage!

b Tu as fait bon voyage?

c Ça va?

d On y va!

e Ça va bien. Et toi?

2b Regarde encore. C'est dans quel ordre?
Watch again. In which order do you hear them mentioned?

SNCF
The *Société Nationale des Chemins de Fer* français is the French national railway system.

Départ En classe

• Classroom language, pronunciation

a C'est quelle page, s'il vous plaît?

d Vous pouvez répéter, s'il vous plaît?

b Je peux avoir un stylo, s'il te plaît?

c Madame/Monsieur, je n'ai pas fini!

e Je suis désolée. J'ai oublié mon livre.

1 **Lis et écoute. Tu entends les bulles a–e dans quel ordre?**
Read and listen. In which order do you hear the bubbles?

Exemple *1 = e*

2 **Relie.**
Match the English (on the right) and the French.

Exemple *a = 2*

1 Could you repeat that, please?
2 Which page is it, please?
3 I'm sorry, I've forgotten my book.
4 Could I have a pen, please?
5 I haven't finished.

3 **Dis les phrases 1–5 en français. Ne regarde pas les bulles!**

4a **Relie et fais d'autres phrases.**

Exemple *C'est quel... exercice, s'il vous plaît?*

a C'est quel...   compris.
b C'est quoi...   exercice, s'il vous plaît?
c Je peux avoir...   m'aider, s'il vous plaît?
d Je n'ai pas...   en anglais?
e Je suis désolé(e), j'ai oublié...   mes devoirs.
f Vous pouvez...   une gomme, s'il te plaît?

4b **Écoute et vérifie.**

A Vowels

 French vowels are short and simple.
Listen and repeat the vowels in this rhyme.

Salade de fruits
a e i o u
a a a ananas
e e e cerise
i i i kiwi
o o o abricot
u u u prune
Salade de fruits
a e i o u!

 Say this line by famous French poet,
Jacques Prévert.

La pipe au papa du Pape Pie pue.

B Accents

 Accents on 'e' change the way it sounds.
Listen and repeat.

e – petit   é – bébé
è – père   ê – fête   ë – Noël

Vive la fête du petit bébé,
Vive la fête du Père Noël!

C Vowel + vowel

 Vowels together make up new sounds.
Listen and repeat the rhymes.

au/eau = o   ai/ei = è   eu; œu = e
oi   ou   oui   ui

Louis le coucou est sous un chou.
C'est rigolo!
La nuit, les étoiles sont sur les toits.
C'est haut, c'est beau!

D Vowel + consonants

 Vowels combine with 'n' or 'm' to make
new sounds.

an = am = en = em
on = om
in = ain = aim = in
un = um

J'ai faim, j'ai faim!
Mange du jambon avec du pain.
J'ai soif, j'ai soif!
Prends un grand verre de jus de raisin!

Bienvenue

The map of Paris is a spiral, a bit like a snail!
The city is divided into **20 districts**: *les arrondissements*.

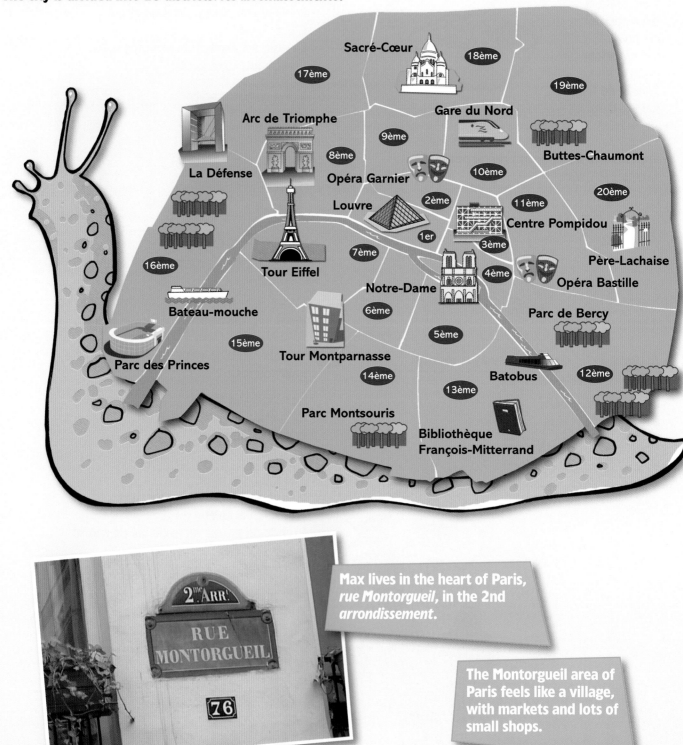

17ème — Sacré-Cœur — 18ème — 19ème

Arc de Triomphe — Gare du Nord — Buttes-Chaumont

9ème — 8ème — Opéra Garnier — 10ème — 20ème

La Défense — 2ème — 11ème — Centre Pompidou

Louvre — 1er — 3ème — Père-Lachaise

16ème — 7ème — 4ème — Opéra Bastille

Tour Eiffel — Notre-Dame — Parc de Bercy

Bateau-mouche — 6ème — 5ème

15ème — Tour Montparnasse — 14ème — Batobus — 12ème

Parc des Princes — 13ème

Parc Montsouris — Bibliothèque François-Mitterrand

Max lives in the heart of Paris, *rue Montorgueil*, in the 2nd *arrondissement*.

2ᵐᵉ ARRᵗ
RUE MONTORGUEIL
76

The Montorgueil area of Paris feels like a village, with markets and lots of small shops.

Context:
Finding out about new places

Grammar focus:
Modal verbs

1 **Regarde les photos. Ce sont quels magasins?**
Match the English and French shop names.

chemist's • baker's • pizzeria

2 **Fais un collage sur ta ville ou ton quartier. Écris des informations.**
Make a collage about the place where you live. Write snippets of information.

● **My neighbourhood**

 1a **Regarde le clip. Max montre le quartier à Joe. Il y a quoi (photos 1–6)?**
Which places (1–6) can you see on the video?

 1b **Relie.**
Match the photos with captions a–f.

Exemple **1b**

 2a **Regarde encore. Note.**
Note the other places you see in the video.

 2b **Cherche dans un dictionnaire bilingue ou le glossaire. Écris: un / une...**
Look up the names for these places and write them down.
Exemple *a post office = une poste*

 3 **À deux: lancez un dé et faites des phrases sur votre quartier!**
Roll a die and write sentences about your neighbourhood.

Il y a...
a **une boulangerie**
b **un supermarché**
c **un bar-tabac**
d **un magasin de sport**
e **un kiosque**
f **un arrêt de bus**

There is / There are...

Il y a	un	kiosque
	une	boulangerie
	des	magasins

There isn't / There aren't...

Il n'y a pas	de	kiosque
	d'	arrêt de bus

Visit **Clic!** OxBox

«Dans ma rue, à gauche, il y a un supermarché.

À côté du supermarché, il y a une  avec des croissants super!

Devant la boulangerie, il y a un **2** .

À droite, en face du kiosque, il y a un **3** .

Derrière l'arrêt de bus, il y a une **4** sympa.

Entre la pizzeria et la **5** , il y a un **6** .

C'est mon magasin préféré!»

Alicia

 4a Lis et complète la bulle d'Alicia.
Read and fill in Alicia's bubble.

Exemple **1** = *boulangerie*

 4b Écoute et vérifie.
Listen and check.

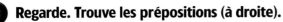 **5 Regarde. Trouve les prépositions (à droite).**
Watch the video and mime the prepositions listed on the right when you hear them mentioned.

à droite	on the right
à gauche	on the left
dans	in
entre	between
devant	in front of
derrière	behind
à côté	next
en face	opposite

 6 À deux: A décrit la rue d'Alicia. B vérifie. (B→A)
A describes Alicia's street from memory and **B** checks with the book.

Exemple **A** *À gauche, il y a une pizzeria.* **B** *Non!*

Défi!

In pairs, prepare a PowerPoint presentation of the neighbourhood around your school.

Example *Dans le quartier de l'école, il y a beaucoup de magasins. Devant l'école, il y a...*

 7a Choisis six endroits pour ta rue. Dessine et écris.
Draw and label six places you think are essential to have in a street.

 7b À deux: A pose des questions. B répond 'oui/non'. A dessine le plan. Comparez! (B→A)
A finds out what's in **B**'s street, draws a plan and then compares with **B**.

Exemple **A** *Il y a une boulangerie?* **B** *Oui.*
A *À droite?* **B** *Non.*

● Knowing what to say

1 Regarde le clip et réponds.
Watch the video and answer the questions in English.

a How does Max greet the lady in the street?
b What does Max tell Joe to say when asking for bus tickets?
c What does Joe say to the man in the shop?
d What does Max say and do when meeting his friend?

2a Lis les expressions 1–4. Relie.
Find 2 French expressions for each English one.

1 Please.   **3** Excuse me!
2 Bless you! **4** You're welcome!

a Excuse-moi!	**b** Excusez-moi!
c À tes souhaits!	**d** À vos souhaits!
e S'il te plaît.	**f** S'il vous plaît.
g De rien!	**h** Je vous en prie!

2b Grammaire: what difference do you notice between the two sets of phrases? Which set is informal?

2c À deux: que dit Mario?
Choose a phrase (a–h) to fill in Mario's bubbles.

1

2 Merci ?

3

4

3 Écoute. Complète avec une expression (a–h).
Listen and add a phrase (a–h) after the beep.

Be polite! Top tips

• Address adults you don't know as **Madame** (woman), **Monsieur** (man) and **Mademoiselle** (young woman).
Use **tu** for a friend, a child or someone your own age.
Use **vous** for adults (unless you know them very well).
Some phrases have different forms: **s'il te plaît** (for **tu**) and **s'il vous plaît** (for **vous**).
• To greet a friend, you can say **Salut!** but to an adult, you say **Bonjour**.
When speaking to an adult, avoid **je veux** (I want) and use **je voudrais** (I would like).

Visit c!ic!

Tu connais les bonnes manières?

Fais le jeu-test! Lis et choisis la réponse a ou b.

You spend a week at your French friend's, Luc Garnier.

1 You meet Monsieur Garnier at the railway station.

   a Salut, monsieur!
   b Bonjour, monsieur!

2 At home, Madame Garnier asks: "would you like some orange juice?"

   a Oui, s'il te plaît.
   b Oui, s'il vous plaît.

3 You and your friend eat at the café. The waiter asks: "What can I get you?"

   a Je veux un sandwich.
   b Je voudrais un sandwich.

4 You help whilst Monsieur and Madame Garnier prepare dinner. They say: "Thank you very much."

   a De rien!
   b Ça va!

5 At the cinema, your friend says: "I'll buy some pop corn."

   a Merci, c'est sympa.
   b Je vous remercie.

6 On your last day, the Garnier family takes you to the station. They say: «Bon voyage!»

   a Salut!
   b Merci. Au revoir!

4 **Lis et fais le jeu-test.**
Read and do the quiz.

5 **Écoute et vérifie.**
Listen to check.

Bonnes réponses: 0–3 = Pas super! Révise les bonnes manières!
4+ = Tu connais les bonnes manières, bravo!

Visit **Clic!** [OxBox]

● Transport

On peut visiter PARIS...

 1 **Écoute. Relie 1–6 et a–f.**
Listen and match the names of transport with the photos.

a **en** bus
b **en** métro
c **en** bateau
d **en** taxi
e **à** vélo
f **à** pied

 WRITING 2a **Ajoute d'autres transports. Fais deux listes: écolo / pas écolo.**
Add other means of transport and make two lists for environmentally friendly and not. Use a dictionary (see page 21).

Exemple **écolo**: *en train*
pas écolo: *à moto, en voiture*

 SPEAKING 2b **À deux: faites un jeu de mémoire. Qui gagne?**

Exemple **A** *Je visite Paris en bus.*
B *Je visite Paris en bus et en métro.*
A *Je visite Paris en bus, en métro et à moto, etc.*

 SPEAKING 3a **Écoute «Tu vas comment au collège?» Note les transports.**
Listen to the survey and note the means of transport mentioned.

 SPEAKING 3b **Sondage en classe: notez les résultats. Écolo ou pas?**
Do the survey in your class and write down the results.

Exemple *11 élèves: à pied. C'est écolo.*

Grammaire

en + most means of transport where you sit inside
à + on foot and on two wheels

Je vais au collège	en	bus / voiture...
	à	vélo / pied...

Tu vas comment au collège?

Visit **Clic!**

Rick est à Paris, chez son ami français Sam.

Rick: Je peux aller à la tour Eiffel à pied?

Sam: Euh, non, c'est loin*! *a long way away

Rick: Je dois prendre le métro?

Sam: Non, tu peux prendre un vélib' si tu veux!

Rick: Un vélib'? Oui, je veux bien!

vélo + **lib**re-service → **vélib'**
= self-service rented bike

 Lis et écoute. Réponds.

Read and listen to the conversation. Answer the questions in English.

a Where does Rick want to go?
b How does he want to get there?
c Is it possible? Why?
d What does Sam suggest?

 Écoute et lis. Complète.

Listen and read the text about the *vélib'*. Fill in
the missing information with the words from the box.

Exemple **1** = *14*

Visite Paris à vélib'!
Pour utiliser le vélib':

1 Tu dois avoir ✳✳ ans.

2 Tu dois mesurer* plus de ✳✳ m. *to measure

3 Tu dois acheter une carte (✳✳ € pour une journée).

4 Tu peux acheter la carte sur ✳✳ ou dans un tabac ou une ✳✳.

5 Tu dois ramener* le vélo à une station: avant *to bring back
✳✳ minutes, c'est gratuit* (après tu dois payer). free

6 Si tu veux, tu peux prendre un autre vélo (pour encore ✳✳
minutes gratuites).

7 Tu peux ramener ✳✳ à n'importe quelle* station. *any

Grammaire

Modal verbs + infinitive

Three very useful verbs:
vouloir = what you want to do
pouvoir = what you can do
devoir = what you have to do

je veux	I want
tu veux	You want
je peux	I can
tu peux	You can
je dois	I have to
tu dois	You have to

Example: **Je veux aller à Paris**. I want to go
to Paris.

boulangerie 30 14 le vélo
Internet 1,50 30

1.4 C'est par où?

• Directions

La Chasse au trésor!

MISSION 1

 Écoute et relie 1–6 et a–f.
Listen and match the instructions to the correct pictures.

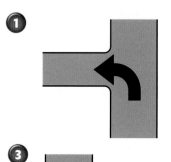

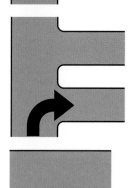
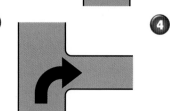

a	**tournez à gauche**	= turn left
b	**tournez à droite**	= turn right
c	**allez tout droit**	= go straight on
d	**allez jusqu'au bout de la rue**	= go to the end of the road
e	**prenez la première rue à droite**	= take the first road on the right
f	**prenez la deuxième rue à gauche**	= take the second road on the left

MISSION 2

 2a READING **Apprends les instructions.**
Learn the instructions by heart. What helps you learn? Listening to them? Writing them? Miming?

 2b Grammaire: écoute. *Tu* ou *vous*?
Listen to the instructions. Which form is used (*tu* or *vous*)?

Grammaire

For an instruction
1 to an adult or several people:
Tournez! *Allez!* *Prenez!*
2 to a friend:
Tourne! *Va!* *Prends!*

Visit clic! OxBox

Le Village au trésor

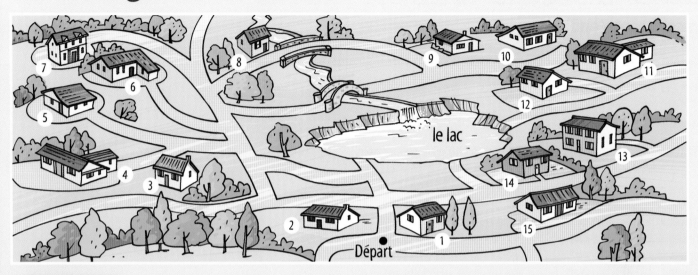

MISSION 3

 3a **Écoute et lis l'Indice 1 pour trouver l'Indice 2 sur la carte.**
Read Clue 1 and work out where to find Clue 2 (numbers 1–15 on the map).

 3b **Trouve le français.**
Find the French for the English link words.

first   then (x 2)   finally

> **Indice 1**
> **Pour trouver l'Indice 2:**
> Tu es au Départ. D'abord, va tout droit. Puis, prends la deuxième rue à gauche. Ensuite, tourne à droite et prends la première à droite. Va tout droit. Pour finir, va jusqu'au bout de la rue. L'Indice 2 est là, à gauche, dans la maison.

MISSION 4

 4 **Écoute l'Indice 2 pour trouver le trésor.**
Now listen to Clue 2 to work out where the treasure is. Follow the directions on the map.

 5 **À deux: A demande le chemin. B répond. (B→A)**
A asks **B** how to get to one of the four places below.
B chooses a location and gives instructions.

Exemple   **A** *Pour aller à la poste, s'il te plaît?*
          B *Alors, tu es au Départ. Va tout droit, etc.*

la poste   le supermarché   le magasin   le restaurant

Pou aller	au	supermarché / magasin / restaurant?		
	à la	poste		
Va	jusqu'au bout de la rue tout droit			
Tourne	à	gauche droite		
Prends	la	première deuxième	rue	à	gauche droite

1.5 Labo-langue

Bien comprendre *Present tense endings + modal verbs*

Present tense endings

In Clic 1, you learned that French verbs fall into three groups.

1 = **-er** verbs (mostly regular) like *aimer*
2 = **-ir** verbs like *finir*
3 = all **other** verbs (irregular): *avoir, être, etc.*

You learned the forms of the verbs in the present tense.

aimer		finir	
j'	aim**e**	je	fini**s**
tu	aim**es**	tu	fini**s**
il/elle/on	aim**e**	il/elle/on	fini**t**
nous	am**ons**	nous**e**	fini**ssons**
vous	aim**ez**	vous	fini**ssez**
ils/elles	aim**ent**	ils/elles	fini**ssent**

1 Copy the diagram and add the verbs below in the correct places. Add a few other verbs of your choice.

adore • mange • choisis • achètes • bois • appelle • joue • parle

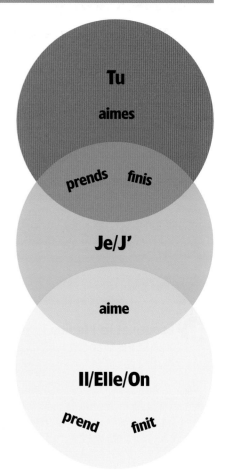

Tu
aimes

prends   finis

Je/J'

aime

Il/Elle/On

prend   finit

Remember to learn some irregulars by heart!

avoir	être	aller	faire
j'ai	je suis	je vais	je fais
tu as	tu es	tu vas	tu fais
il/elle/on a	il/elle/on est	il/elle/on va	il/elle/on fait
nous avons	nous sommes	nous allons	nous faisons
vous avez	vous êtes	vous allez	vous faites
ils/elles ont	ils/elles sont	ils/elles vont	ils/elles font

Modal verbs: *pouvoir / devoir / vouloir*

Use a modal verb **+ infinitive** when you want to say:
- what you can / can't do – **je peux**
- what you want / don't want to do – **je veux**
- what you have to do / don't have to do – **je dois**

2 What is the correct translation?

1 Je veux faire un gâteau. *I can / want to / have to make a cake.*
2 Tu dois prendre le bus? *Do you want to / Do you have to / can you take the bus?*
3 Je ne peux pas sortir ce soir. *I can't / don't have to / don't want to go out tonight.*
4 Elle doit aller au collège. *She wants to / has to / can go to school.*
5 Tu peux venir avec moi? *Can you / Do you have to / Do you want to come with me?*
6 Il ne veut pas prendre le métro. *He can't / doesn't want to / doesn't have to take the tube.*

3a Copy the grid and complete it.

3b Complete the sentences with the right form of the verbs from the grid.

	je	tu	il/elle/on
pouvoir	peux	?	?
vouloir	?	veux	?
devoir	?	?	doit

1 Max, tu **v**✳✳✳ sortir ce soir?
2 **J**e **p**✳✳✳ aller en ville à pied?
3 Je **v**✳✳✳ passer un week-end à Paris!
4 Je **d**✳✳✳ faire la vaisselle.
5 Elle **v**✳✳✳ sortir en ville avec nous mais elle ne **p**✳✳✳ pas: elle **d**✳✳✳ rentrer.
6 Tu **p**✳✳✳ aller au cinéma ou tu **d**✳✳✳ travailler?

Bien apprendre   *Using a dictionary*

When using a bilingual dictionary, remember to check that the words you find are the right ones!
Check examples given in the entry. Is the word a noun, a verb, an adjective, etc.?

READING 1 Choose the correct translations. Check with your French–English dictionary.

The word 'flat' can refer to both **1** the place you live, and **2** an even surface.
In French, you need two different words:
1 *appartement* and **2** *plat*.

French words too can have several meanings.

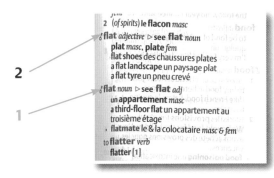

1 It's very <u>flat</u> around here.
C'est très a) **appartement** b) **plat** ici.

2 Do you want <u>ice</u> in your drink?
Tu veux a) **du verglas** b) **des glaçons**?

3 J'ai une <u>pièce</u> d'un euro.
I have a one euro a) **coin** b) **room**.

4 Tu aimes la <u>pêche</u> en mer?
Do you like a) **a peach** b) **fishing** in the sea?

Lis et relie A–D et 1–4.

Read the dialogues and match them to the pictures.

1 – Bonjour, Monsieur. Je voudrais trois vélib', s'il vous plait.

2 – Je peux acheter un ticket de bus?
 – Oui, c'est deux euros.

3 – Mon amie et moi, on veut prendre un vélib', c'est possible?
 – Oui, mais tu dois acheter une carte.

4 – Je peux vous aider, madame?
 – Oui, je veux traverser la rue...

Écoute et chante!

Un kilomètre à pied

Un kilomètre à pied, ça use*, ça use

Un kilomètre à pied, ça use
les souliers*!

Deux kilomètres à pied, ça use, ça use

Deux kilomètres à pied, ça use les souliers!

Trois...

*it wears out

*an old-fashioned
word for shoes

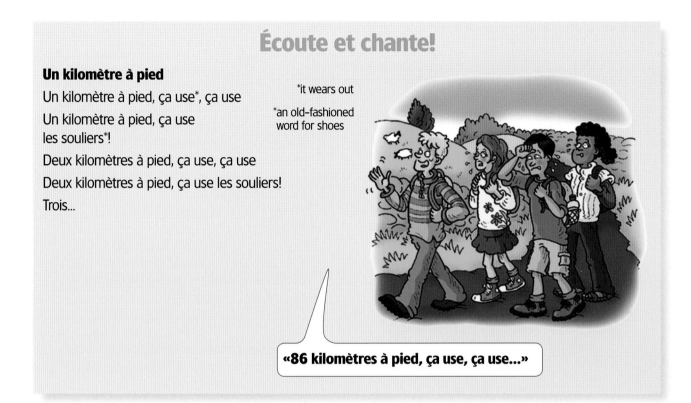

«86 kilomètres à pied, ça use, ça use...»

Virelangue

Dis vite, très vite, trois fois!

Say this very fast three times!

Six cents serpents sifflent!

Proverbes

Relie le français et l'anglais.

Match the French and English proverbs.

1 Quand on veut, on peut!

2 'Impossible' n'est pas français.

3 On promet comme on veut, on tient
comme on peut.

a *Promises are like pie crust, made to
be broken.*

b *Where there's a will, there's a way!*

c *There is no such word as 'can't.'*

Réponses page 147.

1.7 Clic podcast

Rencontre avec... Olenka

Olenka

Parc des Buttes-Chaumont, Paris, 19ème

1 Écoute le podcast. Choisis les réponses d'Olenka.
Listen to Olenka's podcast and choose her correct answers.

1 Tu es de quelle nationalité?
Je suis **a** française. **b** polonaise*.   *Polish

2 Tu parles quelles langues?
Je parle **a** français et polonais.
      b français, polonais et anglais.

3 Tu as quel âge?
J'ai **a** 13 ans. **b** 16 ans.

4 Tu habites où?
J'habite **a** à Paris, dans le neuvième.
b à Paris, dans le dix-neuvième arrondissement.

5 Où est la station de métro ou l'arrêt de bus de ton quartier?
L'arrêt de bus est **a** au bout de ma rue.
      b à 5 minutes à pied.

6 Tu vas comment au collège en général?
En général, je vais au collège **a** à pied. **b** en métro.

7 Tu vas comment en ville?
Pour aller en ville, je prends **a** le bus. **b** un vélib'.

8 Qu'est-ce qu'il y a dans ton quartier?
Il y a **a** un parc, des magasins et des restaurants super!
      b un parc, des magasins, des restaurants et un cinéma super!

2 À toi de répondre aux questions!
Give your own answers to the questions!

Bien parler   *Silent verb endings: -e/-es/-s/-d/-ds/-t/-ts/-x/-ent*

 1a Read and listen to the rap. Can you hear that all the verb endings sound the same?

 1b Say the rap aloud!

> J'aime... tu aimes... il aime,
> elle aime, on aime... aller à Angoulême.
>
> Je veux... tu veux... il veut,
> elle veut, on veut.... aller à Dreux.
>
> Je dois... tu dois... il doit,
> elle doit, on doit... aller à Blois.
>
> Je prends... tu prends... il prend,
> elle prend, on prend... le train pour Caen.

Écoute!

Listen to the directions and list the pictures in the correct order.

Exemple **1 = a**

a b c

d e f

Lis!

Read and decide where each shop is.

Exemple **1** = *la poste*

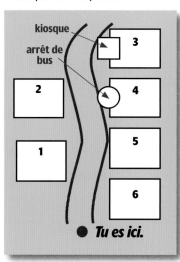

Le premier magasin à gauche, c'est la poste. À côté, il y a un bar. Devant le bar, il y a un arrêt de bus. Derrière l'arrêt de bus, il y a un magasin de sport. Entre le magasin de sport et la boulangerie, il y a une pharmacie.

Parle!

Use the correct phrase to say the phases in the table, to a friend and/or to his dad.

Exemple *Bonjour! (and not 'Salut!')*

say 'hello'		✓
say 'please'	✓	
say 'Bless you!'		✓
say 'excuse me'		✓
say 'thank you'	✓	✓

Écris!

Answer the questions. Write full sentences.

Exemple *Il y a des magasins, un parc et une piscine.*

1 Qu'est-ce qu'il y a dans ton quartier? *Il y a...*
2 Où est ton magasin préféré? *Mon magasin préféré est entre / devant...*
3 Tu vas comment au collège? *Je vais au collège à / en ...*
4 Tu vas comment en ville?

Mon quartier / *Where I live*

Mon quartier	*Where I live*
il y a un / une...	*there is a...*
il y a des...	*there are...*
il n'y a pas de...	*there's no / there are no...*
une boulangerie	*a baker's*
un supermarché	*a supermarket*
un bar-tabac	*a bar which sells stamps and tobacco*
un magasin de sport	*a sports shop*
un kiosque	*a newspaper stand*
un arrêt de bus	*a bus stop*
une poste	*a post office*
une gare	*a railway station*
un café	*a café*

Où? / *Where?*

Où?	*Where?*
à droite	*on the right*
à gauche	*on the left*
dans	*in*
entre	*between*
devant	*in front of*
derrière	*behind*
à côté	*next*
en face	*opposite*

Pour être poli / *To be polite*

Pour être poli	*To be polite*
Salut	*Hi / Bye*
Bonjour	*Hello*
Au revoir	*Goodbye*
Excuse-moi!	*Excuse me!*
Excusez-moi!	*Excuse me!* (to an adult)
À tes souhaits!	*Bless you!*
À vos souhaits!	*Bless you!* (to an adult)
S'il te plaît	*Please*
S'il vous plaît	*Please* (to an adult)
De rien	*Don't mention it*
Je vous en prie	*Don't mention it* (to an adult)
Merci	*Thanks*
Je vous remercie	*Thank you* (to an adult)

Les transports / *Transport*

Les transports	*Transport*
en bus	*by bus*
en métro	*on the underground*
en bateau	*by boat*
en taxi	*by taxi*
en train	*by train*
à vélo	*by bike*
à moto	*by motorbike*
à pied	*on foot*
Tu vas comment au collège?	*How do you get to en ville?*
Je vais au collège...	*I go to school*
à pied / vélo	*on foot / by bike*
en métro / voiture	*by tube / car*
Je prends le bus.	*I take the bus.*
Je peux aller en ville à pied?	*Can I go to the city centre on foot?*
Je dois prendre le bus?	*Do I have to take the bus?*
Tu peux prendre le métro.	*You can take the tube.*
Je veux bien!	*I'd like to.*

C'est par où? / *Which way is it?*

C'est par où?	*Which way is it?*
Pour aller à / au..., s'il vous plaît?	*Which way is it to...?*
Tourne à droite.	*Turn right.*
Tourne à gauche	*Turn left.*
Va tout droit.	*Go straight on.*
Va jusqu'au bout de la rue.	*Go to the end of the street.*
Prends la première rue à droite.	*Take the first street on the right.*
Prends la deuxième rue à gauche.	*Take the second street on the left.*
d'abord	*first*
puis	*then*
ensuite	*then / next*
pour finir	*finally*

Vouloir, devoir, pouvoir / *Want, have to, can*

Vouloir, devoir, pouvoir + *infinitive*	*Want, have to, can* + *infinitive*
je veux + *infinitive*	*I want to* + *infinitive*
je voudrais	*I'd like*
je peux	*I can*
je dois	*I have to*

À toi!

Look at the photo. Use words from the vocabulary list to write a speech bubble for this man.

Ça roule en roller!

Refrain 1

Ce matin, c'est l'enfer:
pas de bus, pas de train,
pas de tram, pas d'métro.
Aïe aïe aïe, comment faire
pour aller au boulot?

En voiture? Pas question.
Ça pollue la nature.
À vélo? Pas question.
Il n'fait pas assez beau!

[Refrain 1]

Et à pied? Non, non, non!
Ça, ça use les souliers!
En roller? Mais bien sûr!
Le roller, c'est super!
Écolo, rigolo
et presto au boulot!

Refrain 2

Ce matin, c'est super:
pas de bus, pas de train,
pas de tram, pas d'métro.
Pour aller au boulot,
le roller, c'est le bonheur!

 Lis et écoute. Il y a combien de transports?
Read and listen. How many means of transport are mentioned?

Héros et héroïnes du présent et du passé!

héroïnes 2

1 Regarde les photos. Tu connais les personnages?
Can you name any of the models in the photos?

2 Trouve quelqu'un qui...
Find in the photos someone who...

a   est rousse
b   est grand
c   a les cheveux longs
d   est brun
e   est petite
f   a les cheveux raides

3 Crée le musée de tes héros et héroïnes.
Who would be in your waxworks museum?
In groups, make a poster. Cut out or draw pictures and describe them.

Exemple   *Il s'appelle Daniel Craig. Il a les cheveux courts.*

Joe et Nina visitent le Musée Grévin au centre de Paris.

C'est quoi?

C'est un musée avec 300 personnages de cire*.   *wax models

Adresse du musée:
10, boulevard Montmartre – 75009 Paris
Numéro de téléphone: 01 47 70 85 05

Site Internet: www.grevin.com

Ouvert du lundi au vendredi: de 10 h 00 à 18 h 30

Les samedis, dimanches, jours fériés et vacances scolaires: de 10 h 00 à 19 h 00

 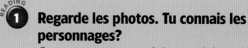

• **Describing people**

1a **Regarde le clip. Tu vois quels personnages?**
Which of these characters do you see in the video? How much do you know about them?

> Charles de Gaulle • Lara Croft • Mozart • Céline Dion •
> Spiderman • Marie Curie • Fabien Barthez • Marie-Antoinette

1b **Regarde encore. Quels métiers sont mentionnés?**
Watch again. Which professions are mentioned?

> un chanteur • un président
> • un joueur de foot • un acteur

2a **Écoute et complète.**
Listen and fill in the missing words.

> Fabien Barthez est footballeur. Il mesure 1,83 mètre alors il est [1], mais il n'est pas trop [2]. Il a les yeux [3]. Il n'a pas de [4] parce qu'il a la tête rasée.

> grand gros
> marron cheveux

2b **Recopie et complète. Explique en anglais.**
Copy the text and add the missing words. Then write in English five facts from the text.

Écoute. Vrai au faux?

Listen to the conversation about General de Gaulle.
True or false?

1 Il est petit.
2 Il est gros.
3 Il a les yeux bleus.
4 Ses cheveux sont blancs.
5 Il n'est pas beau.

 Interviewe ton / ta partenaire sur Céline Dion.

Interview your partner about Céline Dion. Use the photo on page 30. Use *assez* and *très* to make your answers more precise.

Exemple **A** *Céline Dion est comment?*
         B *Elle est assez grande. Elle a les yeux...*

 Lis. C'est David Douillet sur la photo?

Read the bubble and decide if the photo is of David Douillet.

David Douillet *est mon héros. Il mesure 1,96 mètre et il pèse 125 kilos, mais il n'est pas gros parce qu'il est très grand! Il est brun et il a les cheveux assez courts. C'est un champion de judo français, alors il est très célèbre.*

Luc

 Choisis et décris un personnage célèbre (+/- 40 mots).

Choose a famous person and describe them in +/- 40 words. Score at least six points by using linking words.

et, mais, ou = 1 point   **alors, parce que** = 3 points

Grammaire

Adjective alert!

- French **adjectives** must match the noun they describe (masculine or feminine, singular or plural): un <u>acteur</u> **célèbre**, des <u>yeux</u> **bleus**

- There are a few irregular adjectives like:
  beau (m. sing.)   belle (f. sing.)
  beaux (m. pl.)   belles (f. pl.) } = *beautiful*

assez = quite
très = very

Il	(n') est (pas)	grand / gros / beau / petit / mince / brun / blond	
Elle	(n') est (pas)	grande / grosse / belle / petite / mince / brune / blonde	
Il Elle	a	les	cheveux	bruns / blonds / courts / longs
			yeux	bleus / marron / verts
Il Elle	mesure	(1.70) mètres	
	pèse	(70) kilos	

Stratégies

Some useful linking words
To make what you say or write more impressive, use linking words:
et = and
mais = but
ou = or
alors = so
parce que = because

- **What I did last weekend**

1 Relie.
Match the captions to the pictures.

Exemple **a 2**

1   J'ai visité le Musée Grévin avec Nina.

2   J'ai regardé les cartes postales.

3   J'ai acheté un T-shirt.

4   J'ai trouvé un super poster de James Bond.

5   J'ai surfé sur Internet.

6   J'ai mangé un hamburger.

Grammaire

Talking about the past
To say what <u>happened</u> in the past, you need **the perfect tense**:

j'ai visité = I visited (*or* I have visited)
j'ai mangé = I ate (*or* I have eaten)
j'ai acheté = I bought (*or* I have bought)

2 Regarde la fin du clip. Tu entends quels verbes?
Watch the end of the video. Which verbs from sentences 1–6 above do you hear?

Visit **Clic!**

Écoute et note.
Listen and note pictures a–f in the order you hear them.

 Écoute. Présent (Pr) ou passé (Pa)?
Listen and decide if each statement is present (Pr) or past (Pa) tense.

 À deux: jeu de mémoire.
Play a memory chain game with a partner.

Exemple **A** *Le week-end dernier, j'ai surfé sur Internet.*
B *Le week-end dernier, j'ai surfé sur Internet et j'ai acheté un T-shirt.*
A *Le week-end dernier, j'ai surfé sur Internet, j'ai acheté un T-shirt et j'ai joué au foot, etc.*

 Lis. Choisis un adjectif.
Read what Julie did and choose an adjective to describe what she thinks of her weekend.
☺ **génial**   ☺ **pas mal**   ☹ **nul**

 Écris des phrases (a-g).
Write a sentence for each image (a-g).

Exemple a J'ai joué sur ma console.

 Et toi, qu'est-ce que tu as fait le week-end dernier?
What did you do last weekend? Write 3-4 sentences.

Défi!

Give a short speech about your weekend (real or imaginary), using only the verbs on pages 32–33 and in Labo-langue, page 38. Read Labo-langue first for some useful tips too.

Grammaire

To form the *perfect tense*
You need two parts: the present tense of *avoir* + the **past participle** form of the main verb:

j'ai **visité**
tu as **acheté**
il/elle/on a **acheté**

To make the past participle of **regular -er verbs**, replace the **-er** infinitive ending with **-é**:

regard~~er~~ → regard → regard**é**

Le week-end dernier   **Julie Lemoine**

Samedi matin, j'ai écouté la radio et j'ai fait mes devoirs. J'ai mangé une pizza à midi – j'ai bien aimé!
L'après-midi, en ville, j'ai acheté un magazine et j'ai trouvé un DVD super. Le soir, j'ai regardé mon DVD (super bien!) et j'ai regardé un peu la télé. Dimanche, j'ai joué du piano parce que j'ai un examen jeudi, et j'ai joué sur ma console avec une copine.

Le week-end dernier		
j'ai	acheté	des DVD / des magazines / des chaussures / un T-shirt
	surfé	sur Internet
	regardé	la télé / une DVD / un film
	écouté	la radio / de la musique
	mangé	une pizza / un hamburger / des frites
	visité	un musée
	joué	sur ma console / au foot / avec mes copains
	fait	mes devoirs

● Heroes: what they have done

Lilian Thuram

Louis Braille

Jenifer

1 Décris les célébrités.
Describe what the people in the photos look like.

2a C'est qui?
Match a statement to each photo.

a Il a inventé un système qui permet aux aveugles* de lire avec
leurs doigts*.   *les aveugles = blind people
b Il a joué au foot dans l'équipe de France. *leurs doigts* = their fingers
c Elle a gagné la *Star Academy* à la télé.

il a inventé	= *he invented*
il a joué	= *he played*
elle a gagné	= *she won*

2b Écoute et vérifie.
Listen and check.

Visit C]ic! OxBox

> **Tu es fan? Ton héros ou ton héroïne, c'est qui?**
>
> **Qu'est-ce qu'il/elle a fait?**

Bastien, Bruxelles

> **Mon héroïne, c'est la chanteuse française <u>Jenifer</u>. Elle a gagné la *Star Academy* à la télé et elle a eu beaucoup de succès. Elle a fait beaucoup de CD et de DVD! Elle a donné un concert à Marseille l'année dernière.**

Maïa, Cassis

3 **Grammaire: Find the French for:**

> **she won • she had • she did • she gave**

4 **À deux: A pose des questions. B répond pour Maïa.**

A asks Bastien's questions. **B** answers for Maïa.

A Ton héros au ton héroïne, c'est qui?
B Mon héroïne, c'est ...
A Qu'est-ce qu'elle a fait?
B Elle a ....

Défi!

Tu es fan? Réponds aux questions de Bastien (+/- 50 mots).

Are you a fan? Answer Bastien's questions (+/– 50 words) and use linking words. See page 31

Grammaire

Some past participles are irregular:

avoir	→ eu	(j'ai eu, ...)
être	→ été	(j'ai été, ...)
faire	→ fait	(j'ai fait, ...)

More in Labo-langue, page 38.

Ton héros / héroïne,	c'est qui?		
Mon héros / héroïne,	c'est ...		
Qu'est ce qu'	il elle	a	fait?
Il Elle		a	inventé / gagné / joué / donné / fait...

● Describing a period in history

En juin 1940, les Nazis ont occupé le nord de la France.

la zone occupée

l'Allemagne

la zone libre

Beaucoup de Français ont collaboré avec les Nazis, mais d'autres ont résisté. Ils ont écrit des graffiti antinazi.

Vive la France libre

Ils ont coupé les lignes de téléphone. Souvent, les Nazis ont trouvé et fusillé les coupables*.

*shot those guilty

Nous n'avons rien fait.

En 1941, les Français ont organisé la Résistance. Pour garder le secret, les Résistants ont pris des noms de code.

Je suis Hérisson*.

*un hérisson = hedgehog

Charles de Gaulle a quitté la France. Il a trouvé refuge à Londres pour organiser la libération. À la radio, les Français de Londres ont envoyé des messages codés aux Résistants.

«Les Français parlent aux Français... Lucie a les yeux bleus.»

C'est pour nous. On attaque ce soir!

Les Résistants ont attaqué les trains des Nazis. C'était dangereux.

Les Résistants ont aidé les pilotes britanniques à passer la frontière espagnole.

Beaucoup de Français – hommes, femmes, adolescents – ont travaillé pour la Résistance. Les Nazis ont arrêté, torturé et tué beaucoup de Résistants.

En août 1944, les forces armées françaises, britanniques et américaines ont libéré Paris avec l'aide des Résistants.

Vive la France!

Vive la France!

1 **Lis et écoute. C'est quelle guerre?**
Read and listen. Which war is it?

a   the battle of Waterloo
b   World War I
c   World War II

2 **Réponds en anglais.**
Answer in English.

a   What happened in June 1940?
b   What were the people who did not co-operate with the Germans called in French?
c   Name three things people did to show their defiance of the Germans.
d   Why was it dangerous?
e   How did the French help British airmen?
f   Who liberated Paris in 1944?

Les dates
en 1940 = en mille neuf cent quarante

3 **Attention aux accents! Recopie: *a* ou *à*?**
Be careful with accents. Copy the sentences with *a* or *à*.

a   La guerre **a** commencé en 1939. (*World War II started in1939.*)
b   Charles de Gaulle **a** quitté la France et il est allé **a** Londres. (*Charles de Gaulle left France and went to London.*)
c   Il **a** envoyé des messages **a** la Résistance. (*He sent messages to the Resistance.*)
d   On **a** aidé les Britanniques **a** passer la frontière. (*We helped Britons to cross the border.*)

4 **Choisis A ou B pour les mots de la BD.**
Words often have more than one meaning. Choose meaning A or B for these words in the story.

a occupé:
   A occupied = busy   **B** occupied = taken over

b libre:
   A free = not dominated by others   **B** free = at no cost

c refuge:
   A shelter   **B** traffic island

d les forces:
   A strengths   **B** troops

Défi!

Explain in English how some ordinary French people became involved in the war.

Bien comprendre *Perfect tense verbs with avoir*

> J'ai vu un film d'horreur.
> regardé
> J'ai eu peur!

What tense do I need to talk about things that happened in the past?
The most common past tense is the perfect (*le passé composé*).

How do I form the perfect tense?
You need two parts:
the present tense of *avoir* + **past participle**
  j'_ai_ **visité**
  tu _as_ **acheté**, etc.

How do I know what the past participle is?
To make the past participle of regular **-er** verbs, replace the **-er** infinitive ending with **-é**:

regarder	→	regard	→	regard**é**
parler	→	parl	→	parl**é**
manger	→	mang	→	mang**é**

There are also patterns for regular verbs with infinitives ending **-ir** and **-re**:
-ir verbs: finir → fin + i → fin**i**
-re verbs: vendre → vend + u → vend**u**

Are there any irregular past participles?

⚠ Yes! Many common verbs do not have regular past participles. You need to learn them by heart:

avoir → eu | faire → fait

1 **Which are the perfect tense verbs?**

j'ai parlé
on regarde   nous jouons
il a inventé   elle a fini
elle aime   je visite

2 **Copy and complete with past participles.**
Example *J'ai [lire] le livre. = J'ai lu le livre.*

a Samedi, j'ai [**visiter**] Paris.
b On a [**acheter**] des cartes postales.
c J'ai [**adorer**] les grands magasins.
d Nous avons [**visiter**] tous les monuments.
e J'ai [**préférer**] la tour Eiffel.
f Ma mère a [**faire**] beaucoup de photos.

3 **Translate into English.**

a Nicolas Conté a inventé le crayon.
b Audrey Tautou a joué le rôle d'Amélie Poulain.
c Alexandre Dumas a écrit *Les Trois Mousquetaires*.
d Jean-Baptiste Maunier a chanté dans le film *Les Choristes*.
e René Goscinny a fait les illustrations pour Astérix.
f Jenifer a fait un grand nombre de CD.

Jean-Baptiste Maunier

Bien apprendre   *Improving what you say*

Vous avez un héros ou une héroïne?

Oui, j'ai un héros. Il s'appelle Nicolas Vanier. Il est génial! C'est un explorateur qui a fait des expéditions...

Oui, j'ai un héros.

Oui, j'ai un héros. Il s'appelle Nicolas Vanier. C'est un explorateur.

Which of the three answers on the left do you think is the most interesting? There are a number of ways to improve what you say when you speak French.

 1 Put these tips in order to show which you think are most important (1 = most important, 8 = least important).

- Speak clearly and don't mumble.

- Speak with a good accent.

- Use adjectives for added colour.

- Use linking words like *et*, *mais*, *alors* to link ideas.

- Give opinions (*c'est génial, c'était dangereux*, etc.)

- Make sure you are using the right tense.

- Give examples. Say: *Par exemple...*

- If you don't understand what someone says, say so: *Je n'ai pas compris!*

 2 Discuss with a partner: do you have the same order? Justify your ranking.

 3 Tell your partner in French about a famous person you admire.
Set three of the points above as a target for yourself to improve what you say.

Salut! Je m'appelle Annie. J'ai fait un voyage intéressant, un voyage dans l'histoire, un voyage chez les Romains!

Samedi, j'ai visité l'amphithéatre et j'ai regardé un spectacle de gladiateurs. Je n'ai pas aimé parce que c'était trop violent!

J'ai mangé trois repas par jour: le matin, j'ai mangé du pain, du fromage et du lait.

Le midi, on a fait un pique-nique rapide: on a mangé de la viande et des fruits, et j'ai bu de l'eau.

L'après-midi, après l'école, j'ai mangé de la viande et des légumes avec la famille.

 Lis et décide.
Read and decide whether Annie saw a film about the Romans or travelled back in time.

 Lis et réponds en anglais.
Read and answer the questions for Annie, in English.

a What did you see in the amphitheatre?
b How many meals per day did you have?
c What did you eat in the morning?
d What did you drink at lunch?
e What did you eat at lunch?

 Grammaire: trouve les participes passés.
Find the past participles of these verbs in the text.

boire   *visiter*   *manger*   *regarder*   *faire*   *aimer*

Ça veut dire quoi?

Choisis la bonne réponse.

Il est chauve comme un œuf.

a Il a les cheveux courts.
b Il a les cheveux frisés.
c Il n'a pas de cheveux.

Virelangue

Dis vite trois fois!

Dors-tu, tortue tordue?

Casse-tête

Esope reste ici et se repose.

Cette phrase est magique. Pourquoi?
(Clue! It has something in common with
these words: *elle, Bob, mum*.)

Drôles d'histoires

Joue avec un dé et relie les bouts de phrases correspondants.
Roll a die and make full sentences.

First Throw	Second Throw	Third Throw
1 Un explorateur	1 a fait du canoë	1 dans la jungle.
2 Un Martien vert	2 a fait un voyage en soucoupe volante	2 autour de la Lune.
3 Ma grand-mère	3 a bu du thé	3 dans le salon.
4 Un poisson rouge	4 a nagé trois kilomètres	4 dans la mer.
5 Un voleur	5 a volé une voiture	5 à minuit, dans le centre-ville.
6 Un petit garçon	6 a fait du skateboard	6 dans un parc.

Réponses page 147.

Rencontre avec... Noé

Noé

 **Écoute le podcast. Choisis les réponses de Noé.**

1 Tu as quel âge?
J'ai **a** 13 ans. **b** 14 ans.

2 Tu es grand ou petit?
Je suis **a** assez grand. **b** assez petit.

3 Tu as les yeux de quelle couleur?
J'ai les yeux **a** marron. **b** verts.

4 Tes cheveux sont comment?
J'ai les cheveux **a** courts et raides.
                b longs et frisés.

5 Ton héros/héroïne, c'est qui?
C'est le footballeur **a** Lilian Thuram.
                b Zinédine Zidane.

6 Qu'est-ce qu'il/elle a fait?
Il a joué **a** dans l'équipe de France.
          b dans l'équipe de mon quartier.

7 Qu'est-ce que tu as fait samedi dernier?
J'ai joué **a** au foot. **b** du piano.

8 Qu'est-ce que tu as fait dimanche dernier?
J'ai **a** lu un magazine de sport.
      b regardé un film à la télé.

 À toi de répondre aux questions!

Bien parler   eu, ou *and* u *sounds*

 Read and listen to the conversation on the right. Pay special attention to the different sounds.

 Read the conversation with a partner.

 How sharp is your hearing? You'll hear the man say each word in the pair and then the woman will repeat one of them. Is it A or B?

a	**A** du	**B** deux	
b	**A** joue	**B** jeu	
c	**A** tu	**B** tout	
d	**A** rue	**B** roue	
e	**A** vu	**B** vous	
f	**A** pu	**B** peu	

A reads aloud one of the words. B points to the right word. (B→A)

- Il a les y**eu**x de quelle c**ou**l**eu**r?
- Il a les y**eu**x bl**eu**s.
- T**u** as fait d**u** j**u**do?
- Non, j'ai j**ou**é à des j**eu**x vidéo.

COUCOU!

1 **Écoute!**
Listen and list the pictures in the correct order.

Exemple 1 = **c**

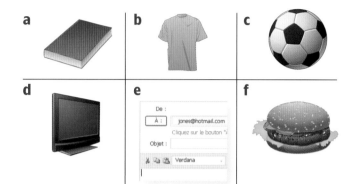

2 **Lis!**
Read the text and write five facts about
Jean-Baptiste Maunier in English.

Mon héros est acteur et chanteur. Il s'appelle
Jean-Baptiste Maunier. Il est né en 1990. Il a
commencé à chanter au collège. Il a joué le
rôle de Pierre Morhange dans le film *Les
Choristes* qui a eu un grand succès en France.

Il est assez grand et mince. Il est brun et il a les
cheveux assez longs.

3 **Parle!**
Describe what one of these people looks like.
Give at least five pieces of information and include
the words *très* and *assez*.
Il / Elle est...
Il / Elle a...

4 **Écris!**
Write about what you did last Saturday
(+/– 50 words). Include answers to the questions
below. Use at least two different linking words.

a Tu as fait du sport? *Oui, j'ai joué au...*
b Tu as regardé la télé? *Oui, j'ai...*
c Qu'est-ce que tu as mangé? *J'ai...*
d Qu'est-ce que tu as acheté?

2.8 Vocabulaire

Mon héros / héroïne	*My hero / heroine*
Il/Elle s'appelle...	*His/Her name is...*
Il est footballeur.	*He is a footballer.*
Il est chanteur / acteur.	*He is a singer / an actor.*
Elle est chanteuse / actrice.	*She is a singer / an actress.*
Il/Elle a beaucoup de médailles.	*He/She has a lot of medals.*
Il/Elle est célèbre.	*He/She is famous.*
Il est grand / petit.	*He is tall / short.*
Elle est grande / petite.	*She is tall / short.*
Il/Elle mesure 1,83 mètre.	*He/She is 1 metre 83 tall.*
Il est gros / mince.	*He is fat / thin.*
Elle est grosse / mince.	*She is fat / thin.*
Il/Elle pèse X kilos.	*He/She weighs X kilos.*
Il est assez beau.	*He is quite good-looking.*
Elle est très belle.	*She is very good-looking.*
Il/Elle a les yeux de quelle couleur?	*What colour are his / her eyes?*
Il/Elle a les yeux marron / bleus.	*He/She has brown / blue eyes.*
Ses cheveux sont comment?	*What is his / her hair like?*
Il est blond / brun / roux.	*He has blond hair / dark hair / red hair.*
Elle est blonde / brune / rousse.	*She has blond hair / dark hair / red hair.*
Il/Elle a les cheveux longs / courts.	*He/She has long / short hair.*
Il/Elle a les cheveux raides / frisés.	*He/She has straight / curly hair.*

Le week-end dernier	*Last weekend*
J'ai visité Paris / le musée.	*I visited Paris / the museum.*
J'ai mangé un hamburger.	*I ate a burger.*
J'ai regardé les cartes postales.	*I looked at the postcards.*
J'ai acheté un T-shirt.	*I bought a T-shirt.*
J'ai trouvé un super poster.	*I found a great poster.*
J'ai surfé sur Internet.	*I surfed the Internet.*
J'ai écouté la radio / un CD.	*I listened to the radio / a CD.*
J'ai regardé la télé / un DVD.	*I watched the TV / a DVD.*
J'ai joué au foot / du piano / sur ma console.	*I played football / the piano / on my playstation.*
J'ai fait mes devoirs.	*I did my homework.*

Tu es fan?	*Are you a fan?*
Ton héros ou ton héroïne, c'est qui?	*Who is your hero / heroine?*
Qu'est-ce qu'Il/Elle a fait?	*What has He/She done?*
Mon héros, c'est...	*My hero is...*
Il/Elle a inventé...	*He/She invented...*
Il/Elle a joué.	*He/She played.*
Il/Elle a fait des CDs / DVDs.	*He/She did CDs / DVDs.*
Il/Elle a eu du succès.	*He/She had success.*

Les mots de liaison	*Linking words*
et	*and*
mais	*but*
ou	*or*
alors	*so*
parce que	*because*
qui	*who*

À toi!

Look at the photo. Use words from the vocabulary list to describe this person.

C'est la vie!

1 J'ai mangé un gâteau énorme
   Maintenant*, je n'suis pas en forme*

   maintenant = now
   en forme = fit

   Refrain

   > Mais j'ai ri
   > Et j'ai dit:
   > C'est la vie!

2 J'ai acheté un p'tit chaton
   Maintenant, c'est un très gros lion

   [Refrain]

3 J'ai travaillé toute la journée
   Maintenant, je suis fatigué(e)

   [Refrain]

4 À la montagne, j'ai fait du ski
   Maintenant, je suis dans mon lit

   [Refrain]

5 Hier soir, j'ai vu un film d'horreur
   Maintenant, j'ai encore très peur

   [Refrain]

---

1 **Lis et écoute. Relie.**
Read and listen. Match each picture to a verse of the song.

READING
2 **Trouve comment on dit:**
Find the French equivalent in the song for:

a I laughed   c that's life
b I said   d I'm still scared

SPEAKING
3 **Chante avec le CD.**
Sing along with the CD.

WRITING
4 **À deux: inventez d'autres couplets.**
In pairs, make up more verses.

Toujours

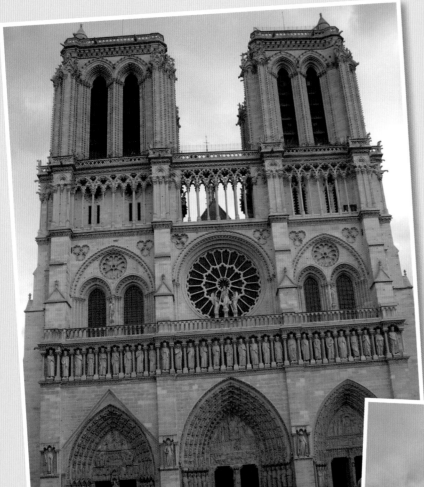

la cathédrale Notre-Dame

l'Arc de Triomphe

la Basilique du Sacré-Cœur
de Montmartre

plus loin! 3

la tour Eiffel

l'avenue des Champs-Élysées

Bienvenue à Paris!

Paris est la capitale de la France.

20 millions de touristes sont allés à Paris l'année dernière.

SPEAKING

1 Que sais-tu de Paris?
What do you know about Paris?
Discuss in groups.

WRITING

2b Décris Paris. Choisis des adjectifs.
Fais un poster.
Describe Paris. Choose an adjective for
each letter. Make a poster.
Exemple **P**assionnant,
Artistique, etc.

P – passionnant, pollué, pittoresque
A – animé, artistique, agréable
R – romantique, relax, riche
I – impressionnant, important, inoubliable
S – spectaculaire, sympa, super

● **A day out; the perfect tense with *être***

Joe à Paris

VIDEO

1a Regarde le clip. Tu vois quels monuments?

VIDEO

1b Regarde le clip. Qui parle: Joe, Max ou Nina?
Who said these phrases and what do they mean?

  a Tu es allé où?
  b On est allés à Notre–Dame.
  c On est montés.
  d On n'est pas entrés dans l'église.

2 Grammaire: écoute. Lève le doigt quand tu
entends un verbe avec *être*.

Grammaire

Perfect tense with *être*
There is a group of verbs that make the
perfect tense with part of ***être*** instead of
avoir. They are usually verbs of movement,
e.g.
venir → **Je suis venu(e)** = I came
sortir → **Je suis sorti(e)** = I went out
See the full list on page 56.

Ma visite à Paris,
par Lucas, 14 ans

Je suis allé à Paris. Je suis parti
samedi dernier. Le matin, je
suis allé à la tour Eiffel.
L'après-midi, j'ai visité le
musée du Louvre. Je suis rentré très tard le soir.
Ma journée à Paris, c'était super!

Ma visite à Paris,
par Chloé, 13 ans

Je suis allée à Paris l'année
dernière. Je suis partie à sept
heures du matin et je suis
arrivée à dix heures. Je ne
suis pas allée à la tour Eiffel – c'était trop cher.
J'ai pris un bus touristique et j'ai vu tous les
monuments. À Paris c'était très intéressant mais
je suis rentrée fatiguée!

3a **Écoute et lis Lucas et Chloé, page 48. Pour chaque personne, note en anglais:**

a when they went to Paris
b what they did
c how we know whether they had a good time

 3b **Grammaire: recopie et complète la grille.**
Reread what Lucas and Chloé said to find verb forms to complete the chart. Mind the endings!

infinitif	masculin	féminin	English
aller	je suis allé	je suis allée	I went
partir			
rentrer			

 3c **À deux: A interviewe B (questions du questionnaire). B est Lucas et répond. Puis B interviewe A (Chloé).**

 4a **Écris des bulles pour Malika et Kévin.**
Use the picture cues and the texts on page 48 to write what Malika and Kévin did. Include answers to the questionnaire.

Grammaire

When the perfect tense is with **être**, the past participle has to agree like an adjective:

il est all**é**   ils sont all**és**

elle est all**ée**   elles sont all**ées**

 When the perfect tense is with **avoir**, there is no agreement.

See Labo-langue, page 56.

Questionnaire

Tu es allé(e) où?

Tu es parti(e) quand?

Tu es rentré(e) quand?

Qu'est-ce que tu as fait?

C'était comment?

Malika: Versailles

octobre

Kévin: en Normandie

août

Je suis	allé(e)	à Paris / au musée etc.
	parti(e)	à dix heures / lundi dernier etc.
	rentré(e) arrivé(e)	tard / le soir / à 10 heures etc. fatiguée
J'ai	visité... vu... pris...	
C'était	super / nul...	

 4b **Écoute et vérifie.**

Visit

- **A place of interest in France; the perfect tense with *être***

Dans l'ouest de la France, il y a un parc d'attractions très original –
Le Puy du Fou.

Il y a des spectacles sensationnels avec des Romains, des Vikings et
des mousquetaires.

En savoir plus: www.puydufou.com

Samedi dernier, **je suis allée** au Puy du Fou
avec ma copine et ses parents. **On** y **est allés**
en voiture et **on est arrivés** à dix heures. **On
est restés** toute la journée parce que c'était
vraiment intéressant.

J'ai vu des spectacles excellents. D'abord, j'ai
vu l'attaque des Vikings. C'était très réaliste.
Mais mon spectacle préféré, c'était le combat
de gladiateurs. **L'empereur est entré** et puis
les centurions sont arrivés et les duels ont
commencé. C'était extraordinaire!

Natacha

D'abord, lis *Bien apprendre*, page 57. Ensuite, fais les activités.

1a **Lis la publicité et le blog de Natacha.
Le thème du Puy du Fou, c'est...**

a les sciences?
b la géographie?
c l'histoire?

1b **Écoute et relis. Trouve le français:**

a There is a very original theme park
b Romans, Vikings and musketeers
c it was really interesting
d my favourite show

je suis tu es il/elle est	allé(e) / arrivé(e) / resté(e) / entré(e)
on est	allés / arrivés / restés / entrés
J'ai Tu as Il/elle/on a	vu / mangé / préféré etc.
C'etait	super / nul / génial etc.

Opinions

C'était...

 2 **Trouve les mots.**

a Le Puy du Fou est dans ✳✳✳ de la France.
b Les spectacles au parc sont ✳✳✳.
c Natacha est allée en excursion avec ✳✳✳.
d Elle a préféré ✳✳✳.
e Au stadium, elle a vu l'empereur et ✳✳✳.

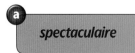
a spectaculaire

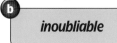
b inoubliable

 3 **Prépare un mini-dictionnaire. Mémorise-le.**
Make a mini-dictionary with any words you learned from the article and the blog. Study the words for a few minutes. Then you and a partner test each other. Who remembers most?

Exemple *un parc d'attractions = a theme park*

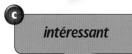
c intéressant

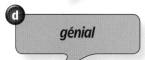
d génial

 4 **Résume les infos sur le Puy du Fou en anglais (80 mots max).**
Summarise the information in English.

e nul

 5 **Lis les adjectifs à droite. (Cherche les mots nouveaux dans un dictionnaire.) Fais deux listes: positifs / négatifs.**

f sensationnel

 6 **Écoute et note les opinions sur le Puy du Fou.**

Exemple *1 = g*

g amusant

h ennuyeux

 7 **Regarde encore le clip vidéo de Joe à Paris. Note les adjectifs / opinions.**

Je suis allé sur Mars.

Défi!

Play 'Consequences' in groups of three. **A** writes the answer to question 1, folds it over and passes it to **B**. **B** writes the answer to question 2, folds the paper and passes it to **C**, etc. At the end, unfold the papers and read aloud.

Questions

1 Tu es allé(e) où?
2 Tu es parti(e) quand?
3 Tu es arrivé(e) quand?
4 Qu'est-ce que tu as fait d'abord?
5 Qu'est-ce que tu as fait ensuite?
6 C'était comment?

Je suis parti le 30 mai.

Je suis arrivé à midi.

D'abord, j'ai vu un spectacle.

Ensuite, j'ai mangé des frites.

C'était amusant!

• Countries and cities; the perfect tense with *être*

Vive l'Europe!

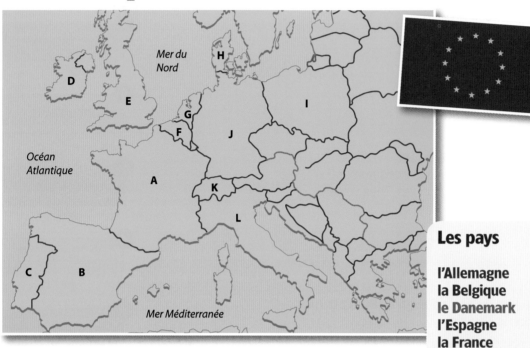

Mer du Nord

Océan Atlantique

Mer Méditerranée

Les pays

l'Allemagne
la Belgique
le Danemark
l'Espagne
la France
la Grande-Bretagne
l'Irlande
l'Italie
les Pays-Bas
la Pologne
le Portugal
la Suisse

 1 Écoute et répète l'alphabet.

 2a Regarde la carte et trouve les pays.

Exemple *l'Allemagne = J*

 2b Écoute et indique.
Listen to 1–6 and point to the country each speaker says they would like to visit.

 2c Ping-pong: A dit une lettre sur la carte et B dit le pays. Attention: *le* ou *la*?

Exemple   **A** *K*
          B *C'est la Suisse.*
          A *Oui!*

 3 C'est où?

Exemple *Paris est en France.*

(Paris) est	en	Irlande / Allemagne / Belgique / Espagne / France / Grande-Bretagne Italie / Pologne / Suisse
	au	Portugal / Danemark
	aux	Pays-Bas

Villes européennes

Amsterdam • Berlin • Bruxelles • Copenhague • Dublin • Genève • Lisbonne • Londres • Madrid • Paris • Rome • Varsovie

Visit **Clic!** OxBox

4 **Lance un dé et fais des phrases.**

Throw a die twice to pick a word/phrase from each column. If they match up correctly, write out the sentence. How many sentences can you make in five minutes?
Exemple

Il est allé aux   *Rome.* ✗

On est arrivés à   *Paris.* ✓

5a **Fais le jeu-test. Choisis a ou b.**

5b **Écoute et vérifie tes réponses.**

First Throw		Second Throw	
 Je suis rentré(e) en		Paris.	
Tu es parti(e) au		France.	
Il est allé aux		Portugal.	
Elle est restée en		Italie.	
Il est venu à		Pays-Bas.	
On est arrivés à		Rome.	

Les nombres

100 – cent
123 – cent vingt-trois
1 000 – mille
3 500 – trois mille cinq cents
1 000 000 – un million
1952 – mille neuf cent cinquante-deux

Grammaire

On est / où On va
à   + town   *(à Paris, à Rome, etc.)*
en   + country (feminine)   *(en France, en Irlande, etc.)*
    + continent   *(en Europe, en Afrique, etc.)*
au   + country (masculine) *(au Portugal, au Danemark, etc.)*
aux + country (plural)   *(aux Pays-Bas, aux États-Unis, etc.)*

Jeu-test: La France, tu connais?

1 **La distance entre la France et la Grande-Bretagne, c'est**
   ⓐ 35 kilomètres ⓑ 53 kilomètres.

2 **Il y a ⓐ 31 millions ⓑ 61 millions d'habitants en France.**

3 **À Paris, il y a plus de ⓐ 10 millions ⓑ 15 millions d'habitants.**

4 **Dans le monde, ⓐ 80 millions ⓑ 160 millions de personnes parlent français.**

5 **En France, il y a ⓐ 101 ⓑ 150 lacs*.**   *lakes

6 **Du nord au sud, la France mesure ⓐ 700 kilomètres ⓑ 1 000 kilomètres.**

7 **ⓐ 200 000 ⓑ 600 000 Français sont d'origine portugaise.**

8 **La Révolution française, c'était en ⓐ 1789 ⓑ 1829.**

● A past holiday; the perfect tense

1a Lis et complète avec le bon verbe.

Léa, 14 ans:

L'hiver dernier, avec ma classe, je suis ⭐1 en vacances à la montagne. On est ⭐2 en février. On est ⭐3 à la station de ski le soir. Le lendemain, on est ⭐4 sur les pistes. On a ⭐5 beaucoup de ski – c'était génial! Mais le troisième jour, ma copine Julie est ⭐6 et est ⭐7 à l'hôpital. Elle est ⭐8 six jours et puis on est ⭐9 en France.

montés   fait   tombée
allée   restée   rentrés
arrivés   allée   partis

1b Réponds en anglais.

a Where did Léa go on holiday?
b Which month did she leave?
c What time of day did they arrive at the ski resort?
d What did she do the first two days?
e Where did she go on the third day? Why?
f How long did she stay in hospital?

Stratégies

Think about what you've learnt!

Where did she go? (*en ville? à la campagne? à la montagne?*)

Which month did she leave? (*Go through the months in your mind and look out for that.*)

What time of day? (*Do you know the French for morning, afternoon and evening so that you can look out for them?*)

2a Recopie le blog de Mathieu en choisissant le bon mot quand il y a un choix.

Je suis / J'ai allé à Biarritz chez mon cousin Olivier.

Je suis / J'ai parti en août et je suis *monté / resté* quinze jours.

Olivier et moi, on *a / est* allés à la plage tous les jours.

J'ai / Je suis fait du surf.

Un jour, on *a / est* allés au musée de la Mer et *j'ai / je suis* vu des requins*.

C'était génial!   *des requins* = sharks

J'ai / Je suis mangé un gâteau aux cerises. **C'était délicieux.**

Mathieu

2b Adapte le blog pour Martin.

Adapt the text in activity 2a to write about Martin. Underline all the words that need to change. Then write out a second text, substituting the new information.

Exemple *Je suis allé à Dieppe chez mon copain Sam.*

Martin:
- went to Dieppe,
- stayed with friend Sam,
- left in July,
- stayed five days,
- went to the town every day,
- played football,
- one day went to the cinema and saw a good film,
- it was great
- ate pancakes.

3 À deux: A pose les questions a–f. B répond pour Mathieu.

a	Tu es allé(e) où?
b	Tu es parti(e) quand?
c	Tu es resté(e) combien de temps?
d	Qu'est-ce que tu as fait?
e	Qu'est-ce que tu as mangé / bu?
f	C'était comment?

partir en août
rester à la maison
aller au bord de la mer
aller au cinéma
visiter un musée
aller en Espagne
manger des gâteaux

Visit **Clic!** [OxBox]

Bien comprendre *Perfect tense verbs with **être***

Some verbs form their perfect tense (the *passé composé*) with part of **être**, not *avoir*, e.g.

je suis allé(e) = I went (*or* I have gone)
tu es allé(e) = you went
il est allé = he went
elle est allée = she went
on est allés = we/they went
ils sont allés = they went (*m. pl*)
elles sont allées = they went (*f. pl*)

They are mostly verbs that indicate movement from one place to another. Try learning them in pairs:

arriver/partir	to arrive/to leave
aller/venir	to go/to come
entrer/sortir	to go in/to go out
monter/descendre	to go up/to go down
rentrer/retourner	to go home/to go back
tomber/rester	to fall/to stay
naître/mourir	to be born/to die

After *être* in the *perfect tense*, the past participle changes. It agrees with the subject of the verb like an adjective (masculine/feminine, singular/plural).

il est all**é**   ils sont all**és**

elle est all**ée**   elles sont all**ées**

Salut! Moi, je suis arrivé hier. Je suis resté mais ma femme est partie. Elle est rentrée à la maison.

1 How many perfect tense verbs can you find in the cartoon? What do they mean?

2 Which past participles in the cartoon go with *être*. Check the list on the left to help you.

3a Write out the sentences, changing the infinitives in brackets into past participles. (Make sure they agree with the subject of the verb.)

Example *Ma cousine [**sortir**]. → Ma cousine est sortie.*

a Anne est [**venir**] chez moi.
b Paul est [**rester**] au collège.
c Mes parents sont [**aller**] au café.
d Ils sont [**retourner**] en France.
e Mon frère est [**tomber**] de son vélo.
f Maman et Julie sont [**descendre**] dans le métro.

3b Translate sentences a–f in activity 3a into English.

Bien apprendre *Reading strategies*

Des vacances actives

Max: Alors, Zoé, qu'est-ce que tu as fait pendant les vacances?

Zoé: Je suis allée en colonie de vacances dans les Pyrénées.

Max: Cool! Raconte!

Zoé: C'était fantastique! J'ai fait du cheval...

Max: Tu t'es bien amusée? C'était difficile?

Zoé: Oui, oui. Faire du cheval, c'est super-dur, surtout la première fois, mais après, ça va. J'ai fait du canoë-kayak aussi, mais l'eau était très froide.

Max: L'eau était froide? Tu es tombée? C'est ça? Ah ah!

Zoé: Oui! Quoi? Ce n'est pas drôle.

- Read the text through fairly quickly at first to get a general sense of what it is about.

 1 **Sum up the dialogue on the left in one sentence in English.**

- Study the title and illustrations. Do they provide clues?

 2 **Name two activities you expect to read about.**

- You don't always need a dictionary.

 3 **List any words in the dialogue that you didn't know before but that you can work out the meaning of.**

- The tense of verbs in a text can affect the meaning.

 4 **Is the dialogue talking about the past, present or future?**

- Every time you read a text, make a note of any new words or phrases you could use yourself.

 5 **Make a note of at least three words / phrases you could re-use.**

Amina et sa sœur Azéla sont nées en France et habitent à Paris. Cet été, elles sont allées en Afrique, au Burkina Faso, le pays de leurs parents. Elles sont restées trois semaines chez leur grand-mère.

Elles sont parties avec leur mère en avril. Elles ont pris l'avion pour Ouagadougou, la capitale. Leur grand-mère a fait un repas typique. C'était génial!

Au Burkina Faso, Amina et Azéla ont mangé du poisson, du riz, des légumes et de la salade.

Amina et Azéla ont fait des excursions dans la région. Elles ont vu des hippopotames. C'était un voyage fantastique!

D'abord, lis *Bien apprendre: Reading strategies*, page 57. Ensuite, fais les activités.

1 Lis et complète les phrases.

a The two girls were born...
b Their parents come from...
c In Burkina Faso, they stayed...
d When they were visiting the region they saw...
e They thought their holiday was...

2 À deux: A pose les questions du questionnaire de la page 55. B répond pour Amina. (B→A)
Exemple *Tu es allée où?*   *Je suis allée au Burkina Faso, en Afrique.*

3 Qu'est-ce qu'on mange au Burkina Faso?

Exemple *fish,..*

Grammaire

Le passé composé au pluriel

	avoir	*être*
ils	ont mang**é**	sont all**és**
elles	ont mang**é**	sont all**ées**

How many examples of these two types of plural verbs can you find in the text? Make two lists.

Sans blague!

Salut! On est déjà sortis ensemble, non? Une ou deux fois?

C'est possible... mais juste une fois... je ne fais jamais deux fois la même erreur.

Ça veut dire quoi?

Choisis la bonne réponse.

Elle est dans la lune.

a She is an astronaut.
b She is very tall.
c She doesn't pay attention.
d She has travelled a lot.

Casse-tête

Thomas a visité quels pays? (Regarde dans un miroir* et c'est facile!)

*mirror

Virelangue

Dis vite trois fois!

Qui est allé à Tahiti cet été?

Réponses page 147.

3.7 Clic podcast

Rencontre avec... Axel

Axel

 Écoute le podcast. Choisis les réponses d'Axel.

1 Tu as visité des pays étrangers?
Oui, je suis allé   **a** en Angleterre et au Canada.
                       b au Canada et en Espagne.
2 Tu es parti(e) en vacances l'année dernière?
Oui, je suis parti   **a** au bord de la mer.   **b** à la montagne.
3 Tu es parti(e) avec qui?
Je suis parti avec   **a** mes parents et mon copain.   **b** ma famille.
4 Tu es parti(e) quand?
Je suis parti   **a** en décembre.   **b** en février.
5 Tu es resté(e) combien de temps?
Je suis resté   **a** une semaine.   **b** dix jours.
6 Qu'est-ce que tu as fait?
J'ai fait   **a** des excursions.   **b** du ski et du scooter des neiges.
7 Qu'est-ce que tu as mangé?
J'ai mangé   **a** de la salade et des légumes.
                b des frites et de la tarte au sucre.
8 C'était comment, les vacances?
C'était   **a** amusant.   **b** nul.

 À toi de répondre aux questions!
Invent answers if you didn't go away last year.

Bien parler   *Intonation*

Intonation is all about how your voice goes up and down as you speak.
The French don't tend to stress one syllable more than another in a
word as we do in English.

 Listen to the words on the right. Are they English (with a stressed syllable) or French (with equal stress)?

 Try to say the French version of the words yourself.

 Listen and note the different intonation for a statement, question or exclamation.

Listen and identify. Write ?, ! or . for each of a–g.

> café ● restaurant ● transport
> animal ● destination ●
> football piano ● souvenir ●
> important information

Stratégies

Intonation for...

a statement   *Max est parti.*

a question   *Max est parti?*

an exclamation *Max est parti!*

Écoute!

Listen to Lucie talking about her holiday.
Answer the questions below in English.

a Where did she go?
b When did she leave?
c How long did she stay?
d What did she do?
e What did she think of it?

Parle!

Describe a day trip to Paris. Say:

- when you went: *Je suis allé(e)...*
- who with: *avec...*
- what you did: *J'ai vu..., J'ai fait..., J'ai visité...*
- what you ate/drank: *J'ai mangé..., J'ai bu...*
- whether or not it was interesting: *C'était...*

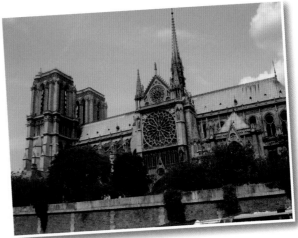

Lis!

Read the dialogue.

a Give the English names of three cities and three countries mentioned.
b Who has been to Britain? When?
c Who skied?
d Who has travelled most?

Ludo:	Tu es déjà allée dans quels pays, Laura?
Laura:	Je suis allée aux États-Unis et au Canada avec mon père. On a fait du ski. C'était super! Et toi?
Ludo:	L'année dernière, je suis allé en Angleterre, à Londres... et à Athènes, en Grèce.
Marc:	Moi, je suis allé à Bruxelles en Belgique, c'est tout. Ce n'était pas super.
Laura:	J'adore les voyages. Je suis allée en Espagne, au Maroc, en Italie,... En Italie, je suis allée à la tour de Pise. C'était génial!

Écris!

Norbert is just back from his holiday.
Use your imagination and write at least
five sentences about it. Include the
details below.

- where/when he went
- how long he stayed
- **what he did**
- what he ate / drank
- what he thought of it

Exemple   *Norbert est allé... Il est monté... Il est
            sorti...*, etc.

3.8 Vocabulaire

Tu es allé(e) où?	*Where did you go?*
Je suis allé(e) à (Paris).	*I went to (Paris).*
Il est allé...	*He went...*
Elle est allée...	*She went...*
Je suis parti(e) en (France).	*I went to (France).*
Tu es parti(e) quand?	*When did you leave?*
Je suis parti(e)...	*I left...*
en décembre	*in December*
le 4 octobre	*on 4th of October*
l'année dernière	*last year*
samedi dernier	*last Saturday*
Qu'est-ce que tu as fait?	*What did you do?*
je suis arrivé(e)	*I arrived*
je suis entré(e)	*I went in*
je suis sorti(e)	*I went out*
le matin	*in the morning*
le soir	*in the evening*
Je suis allé(e) au musée.	*I went to the museum.*
Je suis monté(e) au sommet de la tour Eiffel.	*I went up the Eiffel Tower.*
J'ai vu tous les monuments.	*I saw all the monuments.*
J'ai pris un bus touristique.	*I went on a tourist bus.*
Je suis rentré(e).	*I went back home.*
C'était comment?	*What was it like?*
C'était génial.	*It was great.*

Au Puy du Fou	*At the Puy du Fou*
un parc d'attractions	*a theme park*
Je suis allé à... avec ma copine.	*I went to... with my friend.*
On est allés en voiture.	*We went by car.*
On est arrivés à 10 heures.	*We arrived at 10 o'clock.*
On est restés toute la journée.	*We stayed all day.*
un spectacle	*a performance, show*
Mon spectacle préféré, c'était...	*My favourite show was...*
d'abord	*first of all*
ensuite / puis	*then*

Opinions	*Opinions*
C'était...	*It was...*
très	*very*
vraiment	*really*
amusant	*fun*
ennuyeux	*boring*
génial	*great*
extraordinaire	*extraordinary*
inoubliable	*unforgettable*
intéressant	*interesting*
nul	*rubbish*
sensationnel	*sensational*
spectaculaire	*spectacular*

Les pays	*Countries*
l'Europe	*Europe*
l'Allemagne	*Germany*
la Belgique	*Belgium*
le Danemark	*Denmark*
l'Espagne	*Spain*
la France	*France*
la Grande-Bretagne	*Great Britain*
l'Irlande	*Ireland*
l'Italie	*Italy*
les Pays-Bas	*Netherlands*
la Pologne	*Poland*
le Portugal	*Portugal*
la Suisse	*Switzerland*
Paris est en France.	*Paris is in France.*
Je suis allé(e) en Irlande / au Canada / aux Pays-Bas.	*I went to Ireland / to Canada / to the Netherlands.*
les habitants	*the inhabitants*
un lac	*a lake*

En vacances / On holiday

En vacances	On holiday
J'ai mangé des crêpes.	I ate pancakes.
Je suis allé(e) à la montagne.	I went to the mountains.
au bord de la mer	to the seaside
Tu es parti(e) avec qui?	Who did you go with?
Je suis parti(e) avec mon collège.	I went with my school.
On est partis en février.	We left in February.
On est arrivés à la station de ski.	We arrived at the ski resort.
On est tombés.	We fell over.
Je suis allé(e) à la plage.	I went to the beach.
J'ai vu des requins.	I saw sharks.

À toi!

Look at the photo. Use words from the vocabulary list to help you find three things Léa might say about her recent school trip.

Quel voyage!

1 Je suis parti(e) de Paris.
Je suis arrivé(e) **à Tahiti**.

Refrain   Je suis entré(e), je suis sorti(e),
Je suis allé(e), je suis venu(e),
Je suis monté(e), je suis descendu(e),
Je suis tombé(e) – aïe, aïe, aïe!
Je suis resté(e) deux jours au lit
et je suis rentré(e) à Paris.

2 Je suis parti(e) de Paris.
Je suis arrivé(e) **en Italie**.

[Refrain]

3 Je suis parti(e) de Paris.
Je suis arrivé(e) **en Australie**.

[Refrain]

4 Je suis parti(e) de Paris.
Je suis arrivé(e) **à Tripoli**.

[Refrain]

*Je suis parti(e) de Tripoli.
Et je suis rentré(e) à Paris.*

 Lis et écoute.
Listen and explain why these holidays didn't end happily.

 Relis. Dessine un symbole pour chaque verbe.
Exemple

= Je suis parti(e) de Paris.

Paris

 Chante avec le CD.

Planète

Max, Joe and Nina go shopping.
Nina loves *le Goéland*, a clothes shop in
rue Keller, **11**th *arrondissement*.

mode!

un T-shirt

une casquette

un sweat à capuche

Contexts:
Clothes and fashion

Grammar focus:
Gender and number

Many French teenagers wear designer clothes to go to school.

French clothes shops stay open later than in the UK (7 or 8 pm) but many close a couple of hours for lunch. Most are closed on Sundays, although this is changing in larger towns.

SPEAKING
1 C'est quoi, ton magasin de vêtements préféré?

WRITING
2 C'est quoi, tes vêtements préférés? Fais un poster: dessine ou colle des photos.

● Clothes I like; opinions

 Regarde le clip. Tu vois quels vêtements (a–l)?
Which items of clothing can you see on the video?

 Regarde encore. Note les couleurs mentionnées.

2 Grammaire: révise les couleurs!
Look at the colour pyramid on the right. Why do you think the colours are grouped like that?

3 Écoute. Relie les photos (1–12) aux mots (a–l).

Exemple **1d**

4 À deux: A décrit une photo. B trouve la photo. (B→A)

Exemple **A** *Un T-shirt rose.* **B** *Numéro 3...*

Les vêtements

a	un pantalon	g une chemise
b	un T-shirt	h une robe
c	un short	i une veste
d	un sweat à capuche	j des chaussettes
e	un blouson	k des chaussures
f	une jupe	l des baskets

① orange marron

② blanc/blanche violet/violette

③ rouge jaune rose

④ noir/noire gris/grise vert/verte bleu/bleue

Visit *clic!* O×Box

5a Écoute l'intonation et fais deux listes avec les expressions d'opinion:
☺ **J'aime** = j'adore; ...
☹ **Je n'aime pas** = je déteste; ...

J'adore!	Je déteste!
C'est l'horreur!	La classe!
C'est moche!	Trop beau / belle / cool!
Bof, pas terrible!	Nul / Nulle!

5b **Regarde le clip. Tu entends quelles expressions d'opinion? Tu vois quels gestes ou quelles expressions?**
Watch the clip and note which opinion phrases you hear. What gestures or facial expressions accompany them?

6a **Relie chaque bulle (a–c) à une photo (1–3).**

a Super, **ce** jean! J'adore!

b Nulle, **cette** chemise blanche!

c Bof, pas terribles, **ces** baskets bleues et blanches!

6b **Grammaire: complète a–c avec** ce / cette / ces **et d–f avec un nom de vêtement.**

a Hyper moches, ✳✳✳ chaussettes jaunes.
b Nulle, ✳✳✳ jupe verte!
c Il est trop beau, ✳✳✳ pantalon baggy!
d Cool, **ce** ✳✳✳ ! J'adore!
e Moi, je trouve **cette** ✳✳✳ très classe!
f J'aime beaucoup **ces** ✳✳✳.

Grammaire

	masculine	feminine	plural
this / that	ce (**cet** + noun starting with vowel or h)	cette	ces

7 **À deux: Morpion.**
Play Three in a Row with the grid, page 66. To secure a square, use a phrase above, ce / cette / ces and the right intonation and facial expression or gesture!

Exemple Trop cool, cette robe jaune!

J'adore ce jean!
Cool, cette jupe!
Je déteste ces baskets!
Trop beau, ce pantaloon!

● **My favourite look**

le maquillage

un piercing

le vernis à ongles

A Amélie, *gothique*

une casquette

des lunettes de soleil

un collier

une bague

un collier

des tongs

B Julien, *rappeur*

C Oscar, *surfeur*

 1 **Écoute. Qui parle (A–C)?**

 2 **À deux: imaginez les réponses des deux autres aux questions 1–4.**

 3 **Réponds aux questions pour toi.**

Grammaire

My, your, his, her

	my	your	his / her	
masculine	**mon**	**ton**	**son**	style
feminine	**ma**	**ta**	**sa**	tenue
plural	**mes**	**tes**	**ses**	tongs

La mode

1 C'est quoi, ton style préféré?

Mon style préféré, c'est (le style gothique).

2 Tu mets quoi en général?

En général, je mets (un pantalon noir, …).

3 C'est quoi, ta tenue* préférée?

Ma tenue préférée, c'est (des lunettes de soleil, (un T-shirt, …)

4 C'est quoi, ta marque préférée?

Ma marque préférée, c'est (Nike).

Visit c**lic!** OxBox

Quiz-mode: «Tu aimes la mode?»

Choisis la réponse pour toi.

1 Qu'est-ce que tu mets pour rester à la maison?
   a Des vêtements très confortables!
   b Mon T-shirt Armani et mon pantalon slim.

2 Qu'est-ce que tu mets pour aller à une fête?
   a Je mets ce que* je veux.   *what
   b J'appelle mes copains/copines pour choisir une tenue.

3 Avoir un super look, c'est quoi pour toi?
   a C'est mettre ma tenue préférée.
   b C'est mettre une tenue très mode*.   *latest fashion

4 Ta grand-mère te donne 50 euros.
   Qu'est-ce que tu achètes?
   a Une nouvelle paire de baskets pour faire du sport.
   b Des chaussettes et un T-shirt de marque.

Résultats
une majorité de 'a' = Tu aimes assez la mode!
une majorité de 'b' = Tu adores la mode!

 4 Fais le quiz. Tu es d'accord avec le résultat?

 5 À deux: inventez d'autres questions pour un sondage sur la mode.

Exemple   *Qu'est-ce que tu mets pour aller au collège?*
          a *des chaussettes de Tesco*
          b *des chaussettes Armani*

 6 Grammaire: complète les phrases du Top ou flop de la mode.

Exemple   **a** *... les T-shirts de Top Shop.*
          b *... les pantalons baggy.*

a Ce que j'aime, c'est...
b Ce que je déteste, c'est...

● Shopping for clothes; *le / la / les*

VIDEO

1 Regarde le clip. Qu'est-ce que Joe achète?

READING

2 Lis le mini-guide du shopping. Qui parle, le client / la cliente ou le vendeur / la vendeuse?

3 Écoute. C'est quelle photo (A–D)?

Stratégies

Note how there are several ways of saying the same thing.

Mini-guide du shopping

A

Entre!
- **Bonjour! Je peux vous aider?**
- Merci, je regarde.

or

- **Bonjour! Vous désirez?**
- Je voudrais (un T-shirt).

B

Choisis!
- J'aime bien (le short).
- **Vous faites quelle taille?**
- Je ne sais pas.
- **Vous aimez quelle couleur?**

C

Essaie!
- **Vous voulez essayer? Les cabines sont là.**

or

- Je peux essayer?
- **Les cabines sont là, à gauche / à droite.**

or

- Où sont les cabines, s'il vous plaît?
- **Les cabines sont là, à gauche / à droite.**

D

Décide!
- **Ça vous va? Vous le / la / les prenez?**
- Ça me va. Je le / la / les prends.
- C'est combien?
- **C'est 40 euros.**
- Je ne le / la / les prends pas. C'est trop grand / petit / cher.

Visit **clic!** OxBox

4 À deux: A est vendeur / vendeuse. B est client / cliente. Inventez une conversation pour les dessins. Utilisez les expressions du mini-guide. (B→A)

Exemple A *Je peux vous aider?*
B *Oui, je voudrais un T-shirt.*
C *Vous faites quelle taille?* Etc.

5 Écoute. Aide ton ami anglais à acheter des baskets.

Vendeur / Vendeuse	Client / Cliente
Je peux vous aider? Vous désirez?	Je voudrais (un pantalon). Merci, je regarde. J'aime bien (le pantalon vert).
Vous faites quelle taille?	Je ne sais pas. Taille (10).
Vous aimez quelle couleur?	Le (bleu).
Vous voulez essayer? Les cabines sont là, à gauche / droite.	Merci. Je le / la / les prends. C'est combien? Je ne le / la / les prends pas. C'est trop petit / grand / cher.

---

a In pairs, write a scene in a clothes shop. Give the sales assistant / customer a personality, e.g. grumpy / pushy.

b Perform your script to the class.

c Evaluate each other's performances, using the phrases below.

Bien! Excellent!

C'est trop court!

C'est amusant.

Il faut parler plus fort!

Grammaire

It / Them

masculine	feminine	plural
le	**la**	**les**
it	*it*	*them*

Je **le** prends. *I take **it**.*

le / la becomes **l'** in front of a vowel or h, e.g. **Je peux l'essayer?** *Can I try it?*

● Childhood crazes

1
les scoubidous

2
les Tamagotchi

3
les Pokémon

4
le hula hoop

5
les Pogs

6
le Rubik's Cube

Quand j'étais petite, c'était la mode du [A], ce cerceau* pour danser. C'était amusant!

*hoop

Quand j'étais petit, c'était la mode des [B], ce jeu avec des petits ronds en carton. C'était rigolo*! *funny

Quand j'étais petite, c'était la mode des [C]. C'était bien pour faire des porte-clés*!

*keyrings

Quand j'étais petit, c'était la mode du [D], ce cube avec six couleurs. C'était agaçant*!

*irritating

Quand j'étais petite, c'était la mode des [E], ce petit jeu électronique avec un animal. C'était génial!

Quand j'étais petit, c'était la mode des [F], ce jeu avec des cartes à collectionner. C'était super!

1 Lis les bulles et regarde les photos. Remplace A–F par le nom des jeux 1–6.

2 Mets les jeux 1–6 dans l'ordre chronologique. Écoute et vérifie.

Write a sentence replacing each fad in its decade. Listen to check.

Exemple **1** *Le hula hoop, c'était dans les années cinquante.*

3 «C'était quoi la mode, quand tu étais petit(e)? C'était comment?» Réponds.

années cinquante

années soixante

années soixante-dix

années quatre-vingts

années quatre-vingt-dix

Grammaire

j'étais = *I was*
tu étais = *you were*
c'était = *it was*

Quand j'étais petit(e), c'était la mode du / de la / de l' / des...	
C'était	bien / rigolo / amusant / agaçant / super / génial / nul

Défi!

In pairs, choose a decade (50s to 90s). Do some research, collect some images / items and prepare a short presentation of its fashion and crazes.

Exemple *Dans les années soixante, c'était la mode des robes courtes. C'était aussi la mode de...*

Bien comprendre *Gender matters*

Knowing the gender of a noun is knowing whether it is **masculine** or feminine.
Is it important to know? YES! Gender matters!

A Gender affects the ending of some nouns.

1 **Who says what?**

Example: *1b*

a Je suis vend<u>eur</u>. c Je suis vend<u>euse</u>.
b Je suis client. d Je suis client<u>e</u>.

B Gender affects words around nouns: the determiners and the adjectives.

2 **Copy and complete the grid with the missing determiners:**

le la les un une des ce cette
ces mon ma mes

	a	the	this	my
m. sing.	un	le	ce	mon
f. sing.	?	?	?	?
pl.	?	?	?	?

3 **Copy and fill in with the forms of the colour adjective in the correct places.**
noir   noire   noirs   noires

> Pour aller à l'école, je mets une jupe ✱✱✱ un chapeau ✱✱✱, des chaussettes ✱✱✱ et des gants ✱✱✱. J'aime être originale!

C Gender affects the past participle when *être* is used to make the perfect tense.

4 Match a sentence to each picture.

a Je suis all**é** faire du shopping!
b On est all**és** au fast-food!
c On est all**ées** au cinéma voir un film sur les humains. Quelle horreur!
d Moi, je suis all**ée** chez le dentiste! Super!

D Gender affects the pronouns you use to replace the nouns.

5 *Le, la* or *les*? Copy and fill in.

a J'adore la jupe jaune. Je ✶✶ prends
b La casquette? Je ✶✶ trouve super!
c Les chaussettes, je ✶✶ mets pour jouer au foot.
d J'ai aussi le T-shirt, mais on ne ✶✶ voit pas!
e J'ai acheté ces chaussures et je ✶✶ mets tous les jours!

Bien apprendre — *Masculine or feminine?*

How do I know if a word is masculine or feminine?

- Always learn new words with the word in front of it (*le / la, un / une*).
- In a text, look for clues!

1 Masculine or feminine?

a Je préfère les <u>vêtements</u> blancs.
b Géniale, l'<u>interview</u> avec Jean-Paul Gaultier!
c C'est l'<u>entrée</u> principale du <u>musée</u>.
d Qui habite dans cette <u>oasis</u>?
e Elle sont belles, les <u>bagues</u>.
f J'aime les <u>chemises</u> bleues.

- There are typical masculine / feminine endings. You already know some.

Typical masculine endings:
-ement, -oir, -ier, -isme

Typical feminine endings (with exceptions!):
-ade, -tion, -sion, -ie, -ette

2 Find and write a word for each of these endings.

Example *un Algérien / une Algérienne*

-ien / -ienne   -teur / -trice
-eur / -euse

3 Add *le* or *la*.

a ✶✶✶ tourisme
b ✶✶✶ cahier
c ✶✶✶ charcuterie
d ✶✶✶ chaussette
e ✶✶✶ miroir
f ✶✶✶ limonade
g ✶✶✶ réaction
h ✶✶✶ télévision

Quoi?
C'est un look et une <u>danse</u>.

Quand?
Ce <u>mouvement</u> est né en 2000, à Paris.

Où?
La Tecktonik est: dans les <u>clubs</u>, à l'école, dans la <u>rue</u>! Il y a des 'battles' entre les <u>danseurs</u> mais les <u>batailles</u> ne sont pas <u>violentes</u>!

Comment?
Un Tecktoneur porte un <u>jean</u> <u>slim</u>, un T-shirt <u>fluo</u>, des baskets. Il met du maquillage et boit du TCK.

 READING

1 Trouve le français dans l'article.
night clubs, dance, street, movement, battles, slim jean, violent, fluorescent, dancers

 SPEAKING

2 La Tecktonik, c'est quoi? Résume en anglais.

Visit **clic!** OxBox

Virelangue

Dis vite, très vite!

Regarde le gros rat
gris à la cravate rouge!

La robe rose de
Rosalie est ravissante!

Sans blague!

Une cliente demande à la vendeuse:
- **Je peux essayer cette robe dans la vitrine*?**

*shop window

La vendeuse répond:
- **Vous ne préférez pas
  l'essayer dans une
  cabine?**

Trop cool,
ta ceinture!

- **Tu as une chaussette blanche et une
  chaussette noire, c'est bizarre!**
- **Oui! Et j'ai une
  autre paire
  exactement
  pareille à la
  maison!**

Casse-tête: Qui suis-je?

J'étais grande avant d'être petite.

Vive les couleurs!

Choisis la bonne couleur!

a voir la vie en **noir / rose** = to be optimistic
b la grande **bleue / verte** = the sea
c un petit **blanc / noir** = a cup of coffee
d les petits hommes **verts / rouges** =
extraterrestrials
e avoir des idées **bleues / noires** = to be
sad

Réponses page 147.

Rencontre avec... Malika

Malika

Nike Paris

 Écoute le podcast. Choisis les réponses de Malika.

1 Pour toi, c'est important d'être à la mode?
  a Oui, j'adore être à la mode.
  b Non, je n'aime pas les vêtements mode.

2 C'est quoi, ton style préféré?
  a Mon style, c'est le style rappeur.
  b Mon style préféré, c'est le style surfeur.

3 C'est quoi, ta tenue préférée?
  a Mon baggy blanc et mon sweat à capuche gris.
  b Mon baggy gris et mon sweat à capuche blanc.

4 Tu mets quoi pour aller au collège?
  a Je mets un baggy, un T-shirt, un pull et des baskets.
  b Je mets un jean et un sweat à capuche.

5 Tu aimes bien faire du shopping?
  a Je n'aime pas aller au centre commercial.
  b J'adore faire du shopping!

6 Tu achètes tes vêtements où en général?
  a Je vais au magasin Nike.
  b J'aime aller à Go Sport ou Décathlon.

7 C'est quoi, ta marque préférée?
  a Ecko ou Karl Kani.
  b Nike, Adidas et Puma.

8 C'était quoi la mode quand tu étais petite?
  a C'était la mode des tubes à la télé.
  b C'était la mode des Teletubbies.

 À toi de répondre aux questions!

Bien parler   *The French 'r'*

 Listen very carefully to the words on the right, first in English then French. Then repeat.

 How sharp is your hearing? Listen and note how many 'r' sounds you hear in each word.

 Try and say this!

Le gros rat gris entre dans la serrurerie.

robe	rose	rouge
car	euro	terrible
super	bar	encore

Stratégies

To pronounce the French 'r', think of the Lo**ch** Ness monster!

Serrurerie

1 Écoute!

Listen and match each garment with its colour.

Exemple 1 = a

2 Lis!

Read the text and answer the questions.

a What look does this boy prefer?
b What does he normally wear? (clothes, style, colours?)
c What is his favourite outfit? (clothes, colours?)
d What else does he use to achieve his favourite look? (3 things)

> Moi, j'adore le style gothique. En général, je mets un pantalon slim noir et une chemise blanche.
>
> Ma tenue préférée, c'est mon pantalon noir, ma veste noire et mes chaussures noires.
>
> Je mets une boucle d'oreille et du maquillage blanc et noir.
>
> Ma marque préférée, c'est New Rock.

3 Parle!

Imagine you are buying one of these items in a shop in France. Act out a conversation with the shop assistant. Look at the box on page 71 to help you.

4 Écris!

Answer the questions. Look at the box on page 68 and the words on page 66 to help you.

a Tu mets quoi pour aller à l'école?
b Tu mets quoi pour sortir
c C'est quoi, ta tenue préférée le week-end?
d C'est quoi, ton style préféré?

Les couleurs	Colours		Mon opinion	My opinion
orange	*orange*		J'adore!	*I love it!*
marron	*brown*		Je déteste!	*I hate it!*
blanc / blanche	*white*		C'est l'horreur!	*It's horrible.*
violet / violette	*purple*		C'est moche!	*It's awful.*
rouge	*red*		trop beau / belle / cool	*really beautiful / cool*
rose	*pink*		bof, pas terrible	*not great*
jaune	*yellow*		La classe!	*Classy!*
noir / noire	*black*		nul(le)	*rubbish / awful*
gris / grise	*grey*			
vert / verte	*green*		mon / ma / mes	*my*
bleu / bleue	*blue*		ton / ta / tes	*your*
			ce / cette / ces	*this / these*
			ce que / qu'	*what*

Les vêtements	Clothes		Mon style	My style
un pantalon	*(pair of) trousers*		C'est quoi, ton style préféré?	*What look do you prefer?*
un jean	*(pair of) jeans*		Mon style (préféré), c'est...	*My (favourite) look is...*
un T-shirt	*a T-shirt*		Qu'est-ce que tu mets?	*What do you wear?*
un short	*(pair of) shorts*		Je mets...	*I wear...*
un sweat à capuche	*a hooded top*		C'est quoi, ta tenue préférée?	*What's your favourite outfit?*
un blouson	*a bomber-style jacket*		Ma tenue préférée, c'est...	*My favourite outfit is...*
une jupe	*a skirt*		C'est quoi, ta marque préférée?	*What's your favourite make / brand?*
une chemise	*a shirt*			
une robe	*a dress*		Ma marque préférée, c'est...	*My favourite make / brand is...*
une veste	*a jacket*			
des chaussettes	*(pair of) socks*			
des chaussures	*(pair of) shoes*			
des baskets	*(pair of) trainers*		Au magasin	In the shop
			Vous désirez? / Je peux vous aider?	*Can I help you?*
Accessoires	Accessories		Non, merci, je regarde.	*No thanks, I'm just looking.*
un piercing	*a piercing*		Je voudrais...	*I'd like...*
le maquillage	*make-up*		Quelle taille?	*What size?*
une casquette	*a (baseball) cap*		Je ne sais pas.	*I don't know.*
une bague	*a ring*		Vous voulez essayer?	*Would you like to try on?*
des lunettes de soleil	*(pair of) sunglasses*		Je peux essayer?	*Can I try on?*
un collier	*a necklace*		Où sont les cabines?	*Where are the fitting rooms?*
			Ça vous va?	*Does it fit you?*
			Ça me va.	*It fits me.*
			Vous le / la / les prenez?	*Will you take it / them?*
			Je le / la / les prends.	*I'll take it / them.*

Je ne le / la / les prends pas.	*I won't be taking it / them.*
C'est combien?	*How much is it?*
C'est trop grand / petit / cher.	*It's too large / small / expensive.*

Avant	**Before**
Quand j'étais petit(e), c'était la mode de...	*When I was young, ...was / were in fashion.*
C'était nul.	*It was awful.*
C'était amusant.	*It was amusing.*
C'était rigolo.	*It was funny.*

À toi!

Look at the photo. What do you think of this style? Use words from the vocabulary list to give your opinion.

La valise des vacances

C'est l'été, les vacances et je pars en voyage.
C'est l'été, les vacances et tu fais tes bagages.
Qu'est-ce que je prends pour partir?
Il faut bien réfléchir.

Ta casquette bleu foncé*? *dark blue
Mets-la dans ma valise!
Ton pantalon rayé?
Mets-le dans ma valise!
Tes lunettes de soleil?
Mets-les dans ma valise! *Yeah yeah yeah*

C'est l'été, les vacances et je pars en voyage.
C'est l'été, les vacances et tu fais tes bagages.

Ta p'tite chemise à fleurs?
Mets-la dans ma valise!
Ton bermuda bleu clair*? *light blue
Mets-le dans ma valise!
Tes deux paires de baskets?
Mets-les dans ma valise! *Aïe aïe aïe*

Ça n'va pas, ma valise, je n'peux pas la fermer.
Ça n'va pas, ta valise, tu dois recommencer.

Ma casquette bleu foncé?
Sors-la de ta valise!
Mon pantalon rayé?
Sors-le de ta valise!
Mes lunettes de soleil?
Sors-les de ta valise!
Ma p'tite chemise à fleurs?
Sors-la de ta valise!
Mon bermuda bleu clair?
Sors-le de ta valise!
Mes deux paires de baskets?
Sors-les de ta valise!

 1 Lis et écoute. Note les vêtements / accessoires.

 2 Trouve:
- you are packing
- flowery / stripey
- put it in / take it out
- dark blue / light blue

 3 À deux: inventez d'autres couplets!

Exemple *Ton T-shirt à capuche?*
Mets-le dans ma valise!
Tes chaussettes rouges et vertes?
Mets-les dans ma valise! Etc.

 4 *Chante avec le CD!*

Contexts:
Sport and a healthy lifestyle

Grammar focus:
Negatives

Quoi? **Des milliers de jeunes font du roller à travers la ville.**

Quand? **Le vendredi soir**

Où? **À Paris**

Orange sports TV – started in 2007 – is a sports channel French people watch on TV, on the Internet or on their mobile phones.

1 **Regarde et lis.**
Give the French names of the sports in the photos.

2 **Mini-dico illustré des sports.**
Build up an illustrated list of sport-related vocabulary. Start with the words from activity 1. Then look up the meaning of the words in the box below and add them. Add to your list as you work through unit 5.

> la pêche • un arbitre
> un joueur • une raquette
> lancer • attraper • match nul

Sondage

Quel est ton sport préféré?

19% **le football**
12% **la danse**
10% **le tennis**
9% **l'équitation**
8% **la natation**

6% **le handball**
5% **le rugby**
4% **la gymnastique**
3% **le volleyball**
24% **autres**

● **Body and sports**

① ③ ⑤ ⑩ ⑪ ⑫ ⑭

② ④ ⑥ ⑦ ⑧ ⑨ ⑬

Tony Parker

Les parties du corps

le	bras
	dos
	genou
	nez
	pied
	ventre
la	bouche
	jambe
	main
	tête
l'	oreille
les	cheveux
	doigts
	yeux (un œil)

Grammaire

Plural nouns

The general rule is to add an **-s** (**un pied, deux pied<u>s</u>**) but not always:

un nez > deux nez
un genou > deux genoux

See the rules for irregular plurals on page 131.

un œil > deux yeux

WRITING

1a **Regarde la photo et écris les parties du corps.**

Exemple *1 = la tête*

1b **Écoute et vérifie.**

SPEAKING

2 **À deux: jouez. (B→A)**

Play 'Read my lips.' **A** mouths the name of a part of the body. **B** says the word aloud and points to the right part.

READING

3a **Quelle description correspond au monstre?**

A: Il a une tête, trois yeux et deux nez. Il a quatre oreilles, six bras et six mains. Il a deux jambes et deux pieds.

B: Il a trois jambes et trois pieds. Il a deux bras, un ventre et un dos. Il a une tête et trois yeux. Il a un nez et quatre oreilles.

READING

3b **Dessine l'autre monstre.**

Visit **Clic!** **OxBox**

READING

4a **Relie les sports a–i aux photos 1–9.**

Exemple *a* = 3

Les sports

a	le yoga	e	le canoë
b	le foot(ball)	f	la gymnastique
c	l'équitation	g	la natation
d	la boxe	h	le ping-pong
		i	le patinage

4b **Regarde les photos. Écoute et note les numéros des photos dans l'ordre mentionné.**

Exemple *9, ...*

SPEAKING

5 **Tu aimes quel sport? Joue au Morpion.**

Play Three in a Row with the sports photos. Say whether or not you like the sport to place your counter.

Exemple ***J'aime bien*** *la natation.* / ***Je n'aime pas*** *la boxe.*

Défi!

Say which parts of the body we use for each of the sports pictured above.

Example *Pour le football, on utilise les jambes, ...*

- What sports I do and when

Les sports

Je joue au basket.
Je joue au foot(ball).
Je joue au ping-pong.
Je joue au tennis.

Je fais du jogging.
Je fais du judo.
Je fais du ski.
Je fais de l'équitation.
Je fais de la musculation.
Je fais de la natation.

1 Recopie la liste de sports. Coche les sports mentionnés dans le clip.

to play a sport = jouer à:
Je joue au football.

to do a sport = faire de:
Je fais   du **judo.**
        de la **natation.**
        de l'**équitation.**

2a À deux: A est l'interviewer et pose des questions. B choisit une personne (a–d) et répond. A devine si c'est a, b, c ou d.

Exemple   **A** *Qu'est-ce que tu fais?*   **B** *Je joue au foot, je fais de la*
         A *C'est a!*   *musculation et je joue au ping-pong.*
                                B *Oui!*

a

b

c

d

2b Lis l'exemple et écris des phrases similaires pour b, c et d.

Exemple *Je joue au football. Je fais de la musculation et je joue au ping-pong.*

Visit **clic!** OxBox

3a Lis la BD. Toto est sportif ou paresseux?

Je fais du jogging **tous les jours**!

Je joue au football **deux fois par semaine**.

De temps en temps, je fais du vélo.

Le mercredi après-midi, je joue au tennis.

Le dimanche matin, je fais de la natation.

Mais je **ne** fais **jamais** d'équitation!

When?
le mercredi après-midi
le dimanche matin

How often?
tous les jours
une / deux / trois fois par semaine
de temps en temps
jamais

Use phrases like these to make what you say / write more interesting and precise.

3b Trouve l'équivalent dans la BD.

a on Sunday mornings
b on Wednesday afternoons
c every day

d from time to time
e twice a week
f never

4 Qui est le plus sportif? Écoute 1–6 et note les sports. Ensuite, réécoute et note les expressions de fréquence.

Exemple **1** *judo – once a week*

5 À deux: vous pratiquez les sports à droite? A interviewe B. (B→A)

Exemple **A** *Tu fais du skateboard?*
         B *Oui, je fais du skateboard de temps en temps.*

6 Explique quels sports tu pratiques et quand. Écris +/- 50 mots.
Use at least three different expressions of time and frequency.

je fais du skateboard
je fais du ski
je jeue au tennis
je fais du vélo
je fais de la gym
je fais du jogging
je joue au foot
je fais de la natation

● Daily routine and healthy lifestyle

1a Relie chaque bulle (a–f) à sa traduction (1–6).

a Je m'intéresse au basket. Je m'entraîne une fois par semaine.

b Je me réveille à six heures trente.

c Je mange des chips et je bois du soda.

d Je me couche avant dix heures tous les soirs.

e Je m'ennuie.

f Je ne fume pas.

1 I'm bored.
2 I don't smoke.
3 I wake up at 6.30.
4 I go to bed before 10 o'clock every night.
5 I eat crisps and drink fizzy drinks.
6 I'm interested in basketball. I train once a week.

1b Relie les réponses a–f aux questions du questionnaire.

Questionnaire

1 À quelle heure tu te réveilles?
2 Est-ce que tu fumes?
3 À midi, qu'est-ce que tu manges?
4 Tu t'intéresses aux activités sportives?
5 Au collège, tu t'amuses en EPS?
6 Quand est-ce que tu te couches?

Grammaire

Reflexive verbs (les verbes pronominaux)

These have a pronoun:
subject **+ pronoun +** verb
je **me** couche = *I go to bed.*

The pronoun changes to match the subject it goes with:
je **me** couche
tu **te** couches
il/elle/on **se** couche

Me, **te** and **se** change to **m'**, **t'** and **s'** before a vowel or an h.
Je **m'**entraîne.

To make a reflexive verb negative:
Je **ne** me couche **pas**.

See also page 141.

1c Écoute et vérifie.

Visit clic! OxBox

2 Écoute et note les réponses de Rachel et Mehdi. Qui a le plus de chance d'être champion(ne)?

Rachel

Mehdi

3 À deux: A interviewe B. Pose les questions du questionnaire, page 88. (B→A)

Exemple **A** *À quelle heure tu te réveilles?*
B *Je me réveille à sept heures pendant la semaine et à neuf heures le week-end.*

4 Grammaire: recopie les phrases. Remplace les infinitifs avec la bonne forme du verbe.

Exemple *Tu [s'amuser] au centre sportif?* → *Tu t'amuses au centre sportif?*

a Je [s'entraîner] tous les jours.
b Je [se réveiller] à sept heures tous les matins.
c Tu [se coucher] déjà?
d On [se préparer] pour le match.
e Marie ne [s'amuser] pas à la maison.

Défi!

What do you do to keep healthy?
Write 4-5 sentences.

Je m'entraîne		le weekend
Je fais	du sport / de la natation etc.	le samedi matin
Je joue	au tennis / au foot	tous les jours
		une fois par semaine
Je mange des fruits / légumes...		
Je vais au collège à pied		
Je me	réveille	à (dix heures)
	couche	
Je	ne	fume pas
		mange pas de chips / frites / gâteaux...
		bois pas de soda / d'alcool...

5.4 Champions de France

● Profile of a French sporting champion

Nom:	Cornet
Prénom:	Alizé
Nationalité:	française
Date de naissance:	22 janvier 1990
Lieu de résidence:	Nice, France
Taille:	1,73 mètre
Poids:	60 kilos
Frères/sœurs:	un frère, Sébastien
Langues parlées:	français et anglais
Couleur préférée:	le bleu
Sport préféré:	le tennis

 1a **Lis la fiche et trouve les équivalents.**

a first name
b date of birth
c height
d weight

 1b **Réponds aux questions pour Alizé.**

Exemple *Comment tu t'appelles?   Je m'appelle Alizé Cornet.*

1 **Comment tu t'appelles?**	*Je m'appelle....*
2 **Quand est-ce que tu es né(e)?**	*Je suis née le...*
3 **Tu habites où?**	*J'habite à...*
4 **Tu es de quelle nationalité?**	*Je suis...*
5 **Tu parles quelles langues?**	*Je parle...*
6 **Tu mesures combien?**	*Je mesure...*
7 **Tu pèses combien?**	*Je pèse...*
8 **Tu as des frères et sœurs?**	*J'ai...*
9 **Quel est ton sport préféré?**	*Mon sport préféré, c'est...*
10 **Quelle est ta couleur préférée?**	*Ma couleur...*

 1c **À deux: A pose les 10 questions à B. (B→A)**
Vous avez combien de points communs?

Visit **clic!** OxBox

Marine Debauve est championne de gymnastique artistique. Elle a eu du succès aux Jeux Olympiques. Quel est le secret de son succès? Elle dit: «Je n'ai jamais oublié l'importance de l'entraînement.»

Laura Flessel-Colovic est la star de l'escrime* française. Cette sportive est double championne olympique et elle a été six fois championne du monde. Son secret? Elle dit: «Je ne veux pas décevoir* ma famille.»

*fencing
to disappoint

Christine Janin est la première Française au sommet de l'Everest. En plus, elle est montée sur le plus haut sommet de chaque continent. Elle dit: «Au sommet de l'Everest, je ne pouvais* rien manger, je ne pouvais rien boire − j'étais fatiguée*.»

*I couldn't
tired

 2a **Écoute et lis. Quelle championne n'est pas allée aux Jeux Olympiques?**

 2b **Lis et trouve comment dire:**

a she was successful
b I couldn't eat anything
c I was tired
d I never forgot the importance of training
e she has been world champion six times

 2c **Explique en anglais ce que tu as appris sur ces championnes. Ecris 2 phrases pour chaque personne.**

Défi!

Find out about another French sporting champion. Write an explanation in English of what he/she has done.

Grammaire

The negative

ne... pas = *not*
Je ne veux pas décevoir. = *I don't want to disappoint.*

ne... rien = *nothing/not anything*
Je ne pouvais rien manger. = *I couldn't eat anything.*

ne... jamais = *never*
Je n'ai jamais oublié. = *I have never forgotten.*

Find out more in Labo–langue, page 92.

Bien comprendre *Negatives*

▲ **To make sentences negative, put ne in front of the verb and pas after it:**

(ne → n' if the verb starts with a vowel or h)

▲ **Other negatives work in the same way:**

ne... rien = *nothing, not anything*
Elle ne mange rien. = *She doesn't eat anything.*

ne... jamais = *never, not ever*
Il ne fume jamais. = *He never smokes.*

▲ **What if...**
- the verb is reflexive?
  Answer: put **ne** in front of the **reflexive pronoun** and **pas** after the verb:
  Je **ne me** couche **pas**.

- it's a perfect tense verb?
  Answer: put **ne** in front of the **avoir or être** and **pas** after it:
  Il **n'est pas** allé au stade.

Cher Pierre

J'habite à Dieppe et je ne m'amuse pas. Je n'aime pas ma ville. Je ne fais rien. Je ne sors jamais. Que faire?

Sophie

1 Find all the negatives in the letter. What do they mean?

2 Spot the two phrases in the box that are **not** negative.

il n'y a pas de match   je n'ai rien   il ne joue jamais
on s'entraîne tous les jours   tu ne t'amuses pas
on y va   ce n'est rien

3 Make these sentences negative using *ne... pas.*
Example *J'aime le tennis.* → *Je n'aime pas le tennis.*

a Je joue avec mon copain.
b Paul va au stade.
c Mes parents sont fatigués.
d Tu t'amuses?
e Mon frère aime le foot.
f Je parle avec le prof.
g On joue au tennis.
h Il invite Marie.

4 Translate into English.

a Il va ne pas aller aux Jeux Olympiques.
b Je ne mange rien.
c Tu ne joues jamais au badminton?
d Tu ne connais pas ma soeur?
e Léa ne mange rien avant un match.
f Je n'aime pas mon collège.
g Luc ne gagne jamais.

▲ **After a negative, *du, de la, de l'* and *des* change to *de* (or *d'* in front of a vowel or silent h):**

Je fais **du** judo. → Je ne fais pas **de** judo.
Max fait **de la** natation. → Max ne fait pas **de** natation.

⑤ Finish these answers.

Example *Luc fait du ski? Non, il ne fait pas de ski.*

a Tu fais du karaté? *Non, je...*
b Laura fait du foot? *Non, elle...*
c On va faire du vélo? *Non, on...*
d Il boit de l'eau? *Non, il boit...*
e Tu manges des chips? *Non, je...*
f Elle fait du skate demain? *Non, elle...*
g Je vais faire de la gym? *Non, tu...*
h Ton frère va faire de l'exercice? *Non, il...*

Bien apprendre *Asking questions*

Useful question words

1 **Qui?**	5 **Quand?**
2 **Quoi?**	6 **Pourquoi?**
3 **Combien?**	7 **Comment?**
4 **Où?**	8 **Quel / Quelle / Quels / Quelles?**

Remember how to ask a question:

1 **add a question mark to a statement:** Elle aime le ski?
2 **start with *est-ce que*:** Est-ce qu'elle aime le ski?
3 **with a question word:** Pourquoi elle aime le ski?

***Est-ce que* is often used as well as a question word:**

Quels sports est-ce que tu pratiques?
Quand est-ce qu'il arrive?

① READING Match question words 1–8 with their English equivalents (a–h).

Example *1d*

a	where?	e	why?
b	how much/many?	f	which?
c	what?	g	when?
d	who?	h	how?

② WRITING Write a question for each sentence.

a Tu fais du roller.
b Il joue au rugby.
c Je vais au bowling.
d Elle fait du skateboard.
e Je mange une glace.
f Je vais au collège à pied.

③ WRITING Look back through unit 5. List all the different question words. Who can find the most?

④ SPEAKING What do you notice about the position of *est-ce que* when it is used as well as a question word?

⑤ SPEAKING Put the words in the correct order to make sentences.

a Pourquoi aimes tu le foot?
b Qui tennis joue au?
c Tu où habites?
d Est-ce aimes tu que les animaux?
e Tu de combien as frères?
f Tu combien de langues parles?

Ah non, j'ai mal aux pieds! Et j'ai chaud.

Aaaargh, j'ai mal au ventre... j'ai envie de vomir!

Oh là là, j'ai mal à la tête.

Ouiiiiiiille! Et j'ai mal au dos... c'est affreux!

Aïe, aïe, aïe! J'ai mal à la jambe.

Alors, c'était bien la randonnée*?   *hike

Oui, super! Mais les autres n'étaient pas sympa avec moi... je ne comprends pas pourquoi!

1 **Lis et trouve comment dire:**

my feet are sore • my back hurts • I've got a headache
my leg hurts • I've got stomach ache

2 **À deux: A mime un problème et B devine.**

Exemple   **A** mimes having a sore knee.
          B *Tu as mal au genou?*
          A *Oui, j'ai mal au genou.*

3 **Relis.**
Read the cartoon again and find two more
expressions that use *avoir*. What do you think they mean?

avoir mal

	masculine	feminine	plural
J'ai mal	**au** dos.	**à la** jambe.	**aux** yeux.
	= *my back aches*	= *my leg hurts*	= *my eyes are sore*

Visit cJic! OxBox

Virelangue

Dis vite trois fois:

C'est Kiriri qui rit.

Ça veut dire quoi?

Choisis la bonne réponse.

Il est bête comme ses pieds.

a Il a mal aux pieds.
b Il est très sportif.
c Il est très intelligent.
d Il n'est pas très intelligent.

Le sais-tu?

Les Français aiment beaucoup le sport... à la télé!
La compétition sportive la plus regardée, c'est le
Tour de France, au mois de juillet. Vive le vélo!

Casse-tête

Les noms de certains sports populaires en France sont des mots étrangers.

Parmi ces sports, trouve:
- 3 d'origine japonaise
- 3 d'origine britannique
- 1 d'origine espagnole

le football   le judo

le karaté   la corrida   le hockey

le jogging   l'aïkido

Réponses page 147.

Ne me fais pas rire!

Hé Toto, on joue au football. Tu veux jouer 'avant'?

Euh... je préfère jouer en même temps que vous.

Rencontre avec… Moussa

Moussa

1. **Écoute le podcast. Complète les réponses de Moussa.**

   1 **Quel est ton sport préféré?**
   Mon sport préféré, c'est **a** le football. **b** le vélo.

   2 **Quelles parties du corps utilise-t-on pour ce sport?**
   On utilise surtout **a** les jambes et les genoux.
   b les mains et les bras.

   3 **Tu pratiques quels sports? Quand?**
   a Je fais du vélo tous les jours.
   b Je fais du vélo de temps en temps.

   4 **Tu regardes souvent le sport à la télé?**
   a Non, je ne regarde jamais le sport à la télé.
   b Oui, je regarde le sport une ou deux fois par semaine.

   5 **À quelle heure tu te réveilles?**
   Je me réveille à **a** six heures. **b** six heures trente.

   6 **À midi, qu'est-ce que tu manges?**
   Je mange **a** une salade.
   b un sandwich et des chips.

   7 **Quand est-ce que tu te couches?**
   Je me couche **a** à neuf heures.
   b avant dix heures.

   8 **Quelles sont tes bonnes résolutions pour garder la forme*?** *to keep fit
   Je vais **a** jouer au foot. **b** faire du jogging.

 2. **À toi de répondre aux questions!**

Bien parler *Tricky sounds*

When pronouncing new French words, remember that some letters and letter-combinations are not the same as in English.

 1a **Read the words in box 1 in English.**

> **Box 1**
> chance ● champion ● maths ● marathon
> quart ● question ● motivation ● nation

1b **Listen to the same words read in French. Work out the pronunciation rules for the sounds:**

   a ch   **c** qu
   b th   **d** ion

 1c **Try to say the French version of the words.**

 2a **Work out how to pronounce the words in box 2.**

> **Box 2**
> **a** un chiffre   **e** la qualité
> **b** un cauchemar   **f** le Mexique
> **c** le thon   **g** la communication
> **d** entre parenthèses **h** conditionnel

 2b **Listen to check.**

Écoute!

Listen to Jannick. Note in English the sports he's tried and the part of the body that hurt afterwards.

Exemple *1 = basket – hand*

Parle!

Use the chart to imagine what Théo would say.

Exemple *Je fais du canoë de temps en temps.*

Théo

every day		x				
2 x a week						x
1 x a week			x			
from time to time	x			x		
never					x	

Lis!

What are the sentences that are part of a healthy lifestyle?

Exemple *a,...*

a Je me réveille plein(e) d'énergie.
b Je ne fais jamais de sport.
c Je fais de la natation tous les jours.
d Je ne fume pas.
e Je me couche à 11 h 30 le soir.
f Je ne mange rien le matin.
g Je mange des chips tous les jours.
h Je mange des chips de temps en temps.
i Je joue au basket le mercredi.
j Je vais au collège à vélo.

Écris!

Write at least five things you do to keep fit and healthy, and when / how often.

Example *Je fais du yoga tous les jours avant le collège.*

5.8 Vocabulaire

Tu fais quel sport?	What sport do you do?
Je fais...	I do...
du jogging	jogging
du judo	judo
du ski	skiing
de l'équitation	horse-riding
de la musculation	bodybuilding
de la natation	swimming
du skateboard	skateboarding
du vélo	cycling
de la gym	gymnastics
Je joue...	I play...
au basket	basketball
au foot(ball)	football
au ping-pong	table tennis
au tennis	tennis

Les parties du corps	Parts of the body
le bras	arm
la bouche	mouth
le doigt	finger
le dos	back
le genou	knee
la jambe	leg
la main	hand
le nez	nose
l'oreille	ear
le pied	foot
la tête	head
le ventre	stomach
les cheveux	hair
les yeux (un œil)	eyes (one eye)

Tu fais du sport quand?	When do you do sport?
Je fais du judo le mercredi après-midi.	I do judo on Wednesday afternoons.
le dimanche matin	on Sunday mornings
tous les jours	every day
une fois par semaine	once a week
deux fois par semaine	twice a week
de temps en temps	from time to time
Je ne joue jamais au foot.	I never play football.
Je ne fais pas de jogging.	I don't go jogging.

Ma journée	My day
À quelle heure tu te réveilles?	What time do you wake up?
Je me réveille à sept heures.	I wake up at seven o'clock.
Qu'est-ce que tu manges le matin?	What do you eat in the mornings?
Je mange des chips.	I eat crisps.
Je ne mange rien.	I don't eat anything.
Je bois de l'eau.	I drink water.
Je m'intéresse au basket.	I'm interested in basketball.
Je m'entraîne tous les jours.	I train every day.
Tu t'amuses?	Do you have fun?
Je m'amuse.	I have fun.
Je m'ennuie.	I'm bored/I get bored.
Je ne fume pas.	I don't smoke.
Quand est-ce que tu te couches?	When do you go to bed?
Je me couche à dix heures.	I go to bed at ten o'clock.

Infos personnelles — Personal details

Infos personnelles	Personal details
Comment tu t'appelles?	*What is your name?*
Quand est-ce que tu es né(e)?	*When were you born?*
Tu habites où?	*Where do you live?*
Tu es de quelle nationalité?	*What nationality are you?*
Tu parles quelles langues?	*What languages do you speak?*
Tu mesures combien?	*How tall are you?*
Tu pèses combien?	*How much do you weigh?*
Tu as des frères et sœurs?	*Have you got any brothers and sisters?*
Quel est ton sport préféré?	*Which is your favourite sport?*
Quelle est ta couleur préférée?	*Which is your favourite colour?*

Les négations — Negatives

Les négations	Negatives
ne... pas	*not*
ne... rien	*nothing*
ne... jamais	*never*

À toi!

Look at the photo. Use words from the vocabulary list to imagine what this person is saying.

Je suis le champion!

Refrain: Le sport, j'adore
Et je suis fort
Tu sais ce que j'aime faire?
Il est le champion!

1 Je ne joue pas au rugby
Je n'ai jamais fait de ski
Mais en skateboard, ah oui
En skateboard, je suis le champion!

[Refrain]

2 Je n'fais pas de canoë
Je n'ai jamais fait de plongée
Mais en skateboard, ah oui
En skateboard, je suis le champion!

[Refrain]

3 Je n'aime pas la natation
Je ne joue pas au badminton
Mais en skateboard, ah oui
En skateboard, je suis le champion!

Je suis le champion!
Je suis le champion!
Je suis, je suis, je suis le champion!

1 Lis et écoute. Quel est le sport préféré du chanteur?

2 Relis. Trouve tous les sports et donne l'équivalent en anglais.
Exemple *le rugby* = *rugby*

3 Chante avec le CD.

4 À deux: inventez d'autres couplets.
Exemple *judo / vélo, football / handball, ...*

le Palais Omnisports de Paris-Bercy

What do French teenagers like doing best?
Being with friends is a hot favourite!
* * *

Incredible but true!
7% of French pupils list homework among their pastimes!

copains 6

Max, Nina and Joe are in the *Parc de Bercy*, in the 12th *arrondissement*. Lots of young people meet up here.

In Bercy Park, there are:
- gardens with lawns
- fountains and sculptures
- a large concert and sports hall
- a cinema
- shops open on Sundays
- and restaurants

Context:
Free time with friends

Grammar focus:
Using pronouns

1 **Il y a quoi pour les jeunes dans ta ville? Fais une affiche.**

une salle omnisport?
une salle de concert?
des jardins?
un cinéma?
des magasins?
des restaurants?

2 **C'est quoi, ton passe-temps préféré?**

Exemple *Mon passe-temps préféré, c'est le/la/les...*

● Free time

1a Regarde le clip vidéo. Max, Nina et Joe sont où? Tu vois quels sports?

1b On parle de quelles activités (A–H)?

A J'écoute de la musique

B je fais du sport

C Je fais du shopping

D je sors avec des copains / copines

E je vais sur Internet

F je regarde la télévision

G je vais au cinéma

H je joue à des jeux vidéo

2 Sondage: les jeunes Français et le temps libre. Écoute et note les résultats dans l'ordre.

Exemple *8* = **E**

3 Faites un sondage en classe: «Qu'est-ce que tu fais pendant ton temps libre?» Comparez les résultats.

A *Qu'est-ce que tu fais pendant ton temps libre?*
B *Je vais au cinéma.*
C *Je sors avec des copains.*

musique   II
sport   ~~IIII~~
shopping   I
copains / copines   III
etc.

Visit Clic! OxBox

4a **Écoute. Qui parle (A–H, page 102)?**

 4b **Réécoute. Complète.**

tous les jours
souvent
de temps en temps
(ne)... jamais
une / deux fois par semaine

a Je joue à la Playstation ✳✳✳.
b Je fais du sport ✳✳✳.
c J'écoute ✳✳✳ de la musique.
d ✳✳✳, je fais du shopping.
e Je ne regarde ✳✳✳ la télévision.

 4c **Adapte les phrases a–e pour toi.**
Exemple a *Je **ne** joue **jamais** à la Playstation.*

 5a **Lis le message d'Alex sur son temps libre.**
Complète avec les mots.

devoirs, matchs, football, musique, sport

Alex, 13 ans

J'adore la ✳✳✳ alors je joue du piano tous les jours. Je joue aussi de la guitare électrique. Le samedi après-midi, je joue dans un groupe. En plus, je fais souvent du ✳✳✳: je fais de la natation deux fois par semaine et je joue au ✳✳✳ le mercredi après-midi. Je joue dans une équipe et on a des ✳✳✳ le dimanche matin. Souvent, le dimanche après-midi, après mes ✳✳✳, je ne fais rien!

 5b **Écoute et vérifie.**

 5 **Trouve le français:**

I play the piano.
I play the electric guitar.
I play in a band.
I play in a team.
I don't do anything!

C'est quand?

 **6** **Et toi? Qu'est-ce que tu fais pendant ton temps libre? Écris un texte comme Alex (activity 5a).**

● **Pocket money**

 nquête sur l'argent de poche

Morgane, 12 ans: Ma mère me donne 20 euros par mois et mon père me donne 10 euros par semaine. C'est assez pour acheter ce que je veux.

Chloé, 15 ans: Mes parents ne me donnent jamais d'argent de poche. Alors, je travaille le samedi. On me donne 50 euros par mois − ce n'est pas mal!

Raphaël, 12 ans: Mamie me donne huit euros par semaine. Ce n'est pas beaucoup et je ne peux pas acheter beaucoup de choses.

Simon, 13 ans: Mes parents me donnent 40 euros tous les mois. Quand j'aide à la maison ou quand je travaille bien à l'école, ils me donnent un 'bonus' de 10 euros − c'est bien!

 1 **Lis l'article. Qui n'est pas content de son argent de poche?**

 2 **Relis l'article. C'est qui?**

a Her parents don't give her pocket money.
b His parents give him between 40 and 50 euros per month.
c His grandmother gives him 32 euros per month.
d Her parents give her 60 euros per month.

 3 **Écoute. Morgane, Raphaël, Chloé et Simon ont combien d'argent de poche?**

 4 **Écris ta réponse au magazine (entre 20 et 30 mots).**

Exemple *Mes parents me donnent de l'argent de poche. Ils me donnent 25 livres par mois. Ils me donnent aussi de l'argent pour mon anniversaire et à Noël.*

Grammaire

Pronouns

me = (to) me
te = (to) you

Mes parents	me donnent	(10) livres par mois / semaine
Mon grand-père Ma grand-mère Ma tante Mon oncle Il/Elle	me donne	de l'argent de poche
		de l'argent pour mon anniversaire / Noël
Ils/Elles	ne me donnent pas	d'argent de poche

Visit **Clic!** **OxBox**

5 Écoute Morgane. Elle achète quoi avec son argent de poche?
Fais trois listes et prends des notes en anglais.

souvent: CDs and DVDs, ...   **de temps en temps:**   **jamais:**

«Qu'est-ce que tu achètes avec ton argent de poche?»

1 **des CD, des MP3, des DVD**
2 **des magazines**
3 **des jeux vidéo**
4 **des places de cinéma ou concert**
5 **des bonbons**
6 **des accessoires de mode**
7 **des livres**
8 **des vêtements**
9 **des affaires d'école**

 6 Fais un sondage sur l'argent de poche en classe. Comparez vos réponses au hit-parade.

Qu'est-ce que tu achètes souvent avec ton argent de poche?
Qu'est-ce que tu achètes de temps en temps avec ton argent de poche?
Qu'est-ce que tu n'achètes jamais avec ton argent de poche?

J'achète	souvent	des CD / des magazines etc.
	des places de cinéma . des jeux vidéo etc.	de temps en temps
Je n'achète jamais de / d'	vêtements / livres etc. accessoires de mode etc.	

Défi!

Write a paragraph mentioning five facts about your pocket money.

1 How much you get   3 What you often / occasionally / never spend it on
2 How often and from whom

Example

J'ai dix euros d'argent de poche. Mes parents me donnent mon argent de poche une fois par semaine. De temps en temps, j'aide à la maison et ils me donnent 5 euros. J'achète des magazines avec mon argent de poche.

Visit **Clic!** OxBox

● **My friends and me**

1a Regarde le clip. Max et Nina font quoi ensemble?

a cinéma   **b** sport   **c** musique

1b Max et Nina sont meilleurs copains. Dans quel ordre entends-tu les raisons?
In which order do they mention these reasons for their friendship?

a They like the same things and do everything together.
b Max thinks Nina's really nice and Nina thinks Max is very cool.
c Nina trusts Max and tells him anything.

Test-amitié
Pense à un copain / une copine.

1
● Au collège, je suis toujours avec lui / elle.
▲ Au collège, je suis de temps en temps avec lui / elle.
◆ Au collège, je ne suis jamais avec lui / elle.

2
● Je vais chez lui / elle très souvent.
▲ Je vais chez lui / elle de temps en temps.
◆ Je ne vais jamais chez lui / elle.

3
▲ Je sors de temps en temps sans lui / elle.
◆ Je sors souvent sans lui / elle.
● Je ne sors jamais sans lui / elle.

4
◆ Je me dispute* souvent avec lui / elle.   *I argue
▲ Je me dispute de temps en temps avec lui / elle.
● Je ne me dispute jamais avec lui / elle.

5
◆ Je n'ai jamais de petits cadeaux pour lui / elle.
▲ J'ai des petits cadeaux pour lui / elle à Noël.
● J'ai souvent des petits cadeaux pour lui / elle.

6
● J'aime les mêmes choses* que lui / qu'elle.   *the same things
▲ J'aime souvent les mêmes choses que lui / qu'elle.
◆ Je n'aime pas les mêmes choses que lui / qu'elle.

7
● J'ai beaucoup confiance* en lui / elle.   *I trust
◆ Je n'ai pas confiance en lui / elle.
▲ J'ai assez confiance en lui / elle.

Commentaires:
une majorité de ●:
Vous êtes inséparables! C'est sans doute ton / ta meilleur(e) ami(e)!

une majorité de ▲:
Vous avez beaucoup de choses en commun. C'est un bon copain / une bonne copine.

une majorité de ◆:
C'est juste un(e) copain / copine, pas ton / ta meilleur(e) ami(e).

Visit **clic!** OxBox

2 Lis le test. Trouve le français:

with him / her	at his / her place
without him / her	as him / her
for him / her	in him / her

 3 À deux: faites le test. Vous êtes d'accord avec le commentaire?

 4 Écoute Bruno et note ses réponses au test.

 5 À deux: imaginez les réponses de Malika.

Exemple *Au collège, je suis de temps en temps avec lui.*
Je vais chez lui très souvent.

Malika et Bruno

 6 Lis ce que Paul dit sur Nathan. Réponds.

a Qui n'aime pas le foot?
b Qui aime la musique classique?
c Qui n'aime pas le shopping?

Paul et Nathan

> Paul: «Mon meilleur copain, c'est Nathan mais je n'aime pas les mêmes choses que lui. J'adore le foot mais il aime le basket. Au collège, je suis toujours avec lui. Je vais chez lui très souvent le week-end. J'ai beaucoup confiance en lui et je ne me dispute jamais avec lui.»

 7 Ecris 4-5 phrases sur toi et un(e) ami(e). Utilise le texte de Paul pour t'aider.

Exemple

Ma meilleure copine, c'est...
J'ai beaucoup confiance en elle.
Je sors souvent avec elle...

Grammaire

Him / Her
lui – *him*
elle – *her*

Use **lui / elle** after:
pour (*for*) – C'est pour lui.
avec (*with*) – Je sors avec lui.
chez (*at*) – On va chez elle?
sans (*without*) – Je sors sans lui!

● Organising an event

Quelle est la nationalité de M. Yamato?

Notre projet

On va faire une mégafête internationale. On va faire des équipes.

<u>Avant la fête:</u>
L'équipe A va voir le directeur pour demander la permission et décider où et quand.
L'équipe B va préparer des affiches.
L'équipe C va fabriquer des décorations (par exemple, des drapeaux).
L'équipe D va préparer un buffet de spécialités internationales.
L'équipe E va organiser la musique.
L'équipe F va préparer un quiz.
L'équipe G va présenter des sports de différents pays (par exemple, le cricket).

<u>Après la fête:</u>
On va ranger!

Mégafête des Langues
le 30 juin au gymnase
12h30 - 16h30

Grammaire

The future
aller + infinitive
Je **vais**
Tu **vas**   Example **On va ranger**.
Il/elle/on **va**
Ils/Elles **vont**

 READING
1 Lis le projet de *Mégafête internationale*.
Mets les images (a–h) dans l'ordre du texte.

Exemple *1* = **h**

Visit c!ic! OxBox

2 Regarde la liste à droite. C'est pour quelle(s) équipe(s)?

Exemple **a** = *équipe A*

 3 Écoute. On parle de quoi (a–f)?

Exemple *1 f*

 4 Lis les messages après la fête. Ils parlent de quelles activités de la fête?

a get permission; decide where and when
b decorate the hall
c organise activities
d publicity
e tidy up the hall afterwards
f sort out the food

1 J'ai joué au cricket. J'ai bien aimé. C'était amusant!

2 J'ai essayé le japonais. C'était super! Je voudrais apprendre le japonais!

3 J'ai mangé du crumble aux pommes. C'était très bon!

4 Je n'ai pas trouvé les réponses mais c'était intéressant!

5 J'ai dansé la salsa et la samba. Je n'ai pas vraiment aimé!

Grammaire

The perfect tense with **avoir**

J'**ai**	mang**é**
Tu **as**	dans**é**
Il/Elle/On **a**	essay**é**
Ils/Elles **ont**	jou**é**
	aim**é**

Défi!

Organise your own International Festival! Work in groups and put in a bid. Prepare a proposal in French, give as much detail as possible and be convincing!

- **mention where and when,** e.g. *On va faire une fête le 13 juillet, entre 12 heures 30 et 13 heures 30, dans la salle de français.*
- **mention all the different activities,** e.g. *On va faire un quiz sur la musique française.*
- **mention who does what,** e.g. *L'équipe B va voir la directrice.*

Bien comprendre *Tenses*

There are 3 main tenses that you need to know.

A **The present tense to talk about what you're doing now or what you usually do.**

French verbs fall into three groups.

1 = **-er** verbs (mostly regular) like *aimer*
2 = **-ir** verbs like *finir*
3 = all **other** verbs (irregular): *avoir, être, etc.*

aimer		finir	
j'	aim**e**	je	fin**is**
tu	aim**es**	tu	fin**is**
il/elle/on	aim**e**	il/elle/on	fin**it**
nous	am**ons**	nouse	finis**sons**
vous	aim**ez**	vous	fin**issez**
ils/elles	aim**ent**	ils/elles	fin**issent**

1 **Write each sentence in the present tense.**
  a On [rester] à la maison cet été.
  b Tu [partir] quand en vacances?
  c Vous [jouer] souvent au foot?
  d Nous [aimer] bien le français.
  e Il [perdre] toujours son portable!
  f Ils [sortir] avec des copains ce soir.

B **The perfect tense to talk about what you did recently or what you've done in the past.**

It is made up of two parts: the **auxiliary** (equivalent to 'have / has') + the **past participle** (played, travelled, etc.).
- The auxiliary is usually *avoir*, but it is sometimes *être*.
  j'ai *joué*   **nous avons** *joué*
  tu as *joué*   **vous avez** *joué*
  il/elle/on a *joué* **ils/elles ont** *joué*
- The past participle of regular verbs ends in *–é, –i* or *–u*:
  jou**er** → *jou**é***   fin**ir** → *fin**i***   vend**re** → *vend**u***
- Many common verbs have irregular past participles that you need to learn by heart. See *Grammaire* page 137.
- A group of common verbs use *être* as the auxiliary, instead of *avoir*. These verbs are mostly **to do with coming and going:** *aller, venir, arriver, partir, entrer, sortir, monter, descendre.* See *Grammaire* page 137.

- The past participle of verbs with *être* has to 'agree' with the subject. If the subject is feminine, add **-e**; if it's plural, add **-s**; if it's feminine and plural, add **-es**.
  Je suis arrivé. *(boy speaking)* Luc **est arrivé.**
  Je suis arrivée. *(girl speaking)* Lucie **est arrivée.**

2 **Write each sentence in the perfect tense.**
  a Il [participer] aux Jeux Olympiques.
  b On [finir] le match à deux heures.
  c Elle [acheter] un nouveau CD.
  d J'[choisir] un gâteau au chocolat.
  e Qu'est-ce que tu [faire] ?
  f J'[avoir] un vélo pour mon anniversaire.

3 **Write each sentence in the perfect tense.**
  a Je [sortir] de la maison.
  b Il [partir] à cinq heures.
  c Nathalie, tu [rester] dans ta chambre?
  d Je [aller] au cinéma.
  e Marc [venir] au concert avec son amie.
  f Je [mettre] un pantalon.

C **The future tense to talk about what you're going to do.**

Use the present tense of aller followed by the verb in the infinitive.
je	vais	
tu	vas	
il/elle/on	va	**+ infinitive**
nous	allons	
vous	allez	
ils/elles	vont	

4 **Copy out each sentence, putting the verb in the future tense.**
  a Je [sortir] avec mes copains ce soir.
  b Qu'est-ce que tu [faire] ce week-end?
  c Nous [voir] un film au cinéma.
  d Vous [regarder] le match de foot ce week-end?
  e Je [aller] chez ma grand-mère en vacances.
  f On [dormir] dans une caravane.

Visit **Clic!** OxBox

Bien apprendre *Improve your written work*

A **Make what you write more interesting. Make longer sentences by using:**

a **pronouns:** moi • lui / elle • le / la / les
b **linking words:** mais • et • parce que
c **time expressions:** souvent • de temps en temps • jamais
d **qualifiers:** assez • beaucoup • très

B **Remember to give your opinion (in the past too).**
☺ j'adore • ☺ c'est pas terrible • ☹ c'était amusant!

C **Also try and use different time words and different tenses when appropriate.**

Hier, j'ai fait...;
Aujourd'hui, je fais...;
Demain, je vais faire...

Q: Qu'est-ce que tu fais pendant ton temps libre?

A: Je joue du piano. Je ne suis pas bon.

 Improve this answer by using the advice in A, B and C!
Example *Je joue du piano de temps en temps.*
***J'aime bien** mais je ne suis pas très bon!* ***Hier, j'ai joué** du piano mais **c'était nul!** **Demain, je vais jouer** pendant une heure*.

 Try and improve these answers. Remember steps A, B and C!

a Je fais de l'équitation. J'ai un cheval.
b Je fais du shopping avec des copines.
c Je joue aux Sims sur la PS3. C'est mon jeu préféré.

Write a personal answer to the question about your free time (35–40 words).

Bien parler *Liaison or no liaison?*

 Listen carefully to the words in blue. What do you notice? Repeat.

un **grand** garçon / un **grand** ami
elles partent / **elles** arrivent
un copain / **un** ami
c'est moi / **c'est** elle
dix minutes / **dix** ans
chez lui / **chez** elle

 Read these sentences aloud. Don't forget the liaisons!

Son avion est arrivé en avance.
Ces gros éléphants sont de vieux amis.
Ils ont des habits dans une armoire.
C'est amusant: on est très à la mode.

 Listen to check.

Liaisons
A word ending in -d, -n, -t, -s, -x, -z + a word starting with a consonant will mean no liaison, e.g. *son père.*
A word ending in -d, -n, -t, -s, -x, -z + a word starting with a vowel or an h will mean a liaison, e.g. *son ami.*

Examples:
son ͜ avion
un **petit** ͜ ami
sans ͜ elle, **très** ͜ utile
ils ͜ arrivent
c'est ͜ ici

La télé et la musique: passe-temps numéro 1 des jeunes Français

Les passe-temps pratiqués au cours des trois derniers mois	Oui	Non
J'ai regardé la télévision.	97%	3%
J'ai écouté de la musique.	97%	3%
J'ai regardé des vidéos ou des DVD.	92%	8%
J'ai utilisé un ordinateur ou surfé sur Internet.	92%	8%
J'ai écouté la radio.	81%	19%
J'ai fait du sport (en dehors des cours de sport à l'école).	78%	22%
J'ai lu (en dehors des livres demandés par un professeur).	77%	23%
J'ai joué à des jeux vidéo.	71%	29%
Je suis allé(e) au cinéma.	65%	35%
J'ai joué à un jeu de société.	59%	41%
J'ai pratiqué une activité telle que la musique, le dessin, la danse...	56%	44%
J'ai visité un musée, un monument, une exposition.	42%	58%
Je suis allé(e) au concert ou au spectacle (théâtre, cirque...)	30%	70%

 1 Lis le sondage.

 2 Recopie en deux listes:
a ce que j'ai fait
b ce que je n'ai pas fait

Exemple **a** *J'ai regardé la télé, ...*
b *Je ne suis pas allé(e) au cinéma, ...*

 3 À deux: A pose des questions sur la semaine dernière. B répond. (B→A)

Exemple **A** *Est-ce que tu as regardé la télé la semaine dernière?*
B *Oui, j'ai regardé la télé.*

Grammaire

The negative in the perfect tense
Je **n**'ai **pas** regardé
Je **ne** suis **pas** allé(e)

Visit Clic! OxBox

Ça veut dire quoi?

Lis l'expression. Choisis la bonne réponse.

Le meilleur ami de l'homme, c'est...

a le chien
b le chat
c le cheval

Virelangue

Dis vite, très vite!

Les amis des ennemis de ton ennemi sont-ils tes amis?

Sans blague!

C'est samedi. La maman de Toto lui donne son argent de poche.

«Voilà ton argent de poche, Toto. Qu'est-ce que tu dis?»
«Euh... Ce n'est pas assez.»

Proverbes

Relie le français et l'anglais.

1 Les bons comptes font les bons amis.
2 L'argent ne tombe pas du ciel.
3 L'argent ne fait pas le bonheur.

a Money won't buy you happiness.
b Bad debts make bad friends.
c Money doesn't grow on trees.

Le sais-tu?

L'argent de poche par an en Europe

Grande-Bretagne	£775
Suède	£697
Pays-Bas	£575
France	£442
Allemagne	£438
Italie	£341
Espagne	£310

Réponses page 147.

CHECKLIST IN THE WORKBOOK Page 16

Rencontre avec... Sandrine

Sandrine

Bénévole* dans un refuge de la SPA (Société Protectrice des Animaux)   *volunteer

 1 Écoute le podcast. Choisis les réponses de Sandrine.

1 Qu'est-ce que tu fais pendant ton temps libre?
a Je travaille à la SPA pour avoir de l'argent le samedi après-midi.
b Je suis bénévole à la SPA une fois par semaine.

2 Tu as de l'argent de poche? Qui te le donne?
a Mes parents me donnent de l'argent de poche une fois par semaine.
b Mes grands-parents me donnent de l'argent de poche une fois par semaine.

3 On te donne combien?
a J'ai 40 euros par semaine.
b J'ai 10 euros par semaine.

4 Tu as un petit boulot?
a J'aide dans le magasin de vêtements de mes parents.
b J'ai 30 euros quand je travaille à la SPA.

5 Qu'est-ce que tu fais avec ton argent de poche?
a J'achète des cadeaux à mes copines et je donne le reste à la SPA.
b Je donne 10 euros à la SPA et j'achète des cadeaux à mes copines.

6 Tu as un ou une meilleur(e) ami(e)?
a J'ai une meilleure amie qui s'appelle Katya.
b J'ai beaucoup de copines et pas vraiment de meilleure amie.

7 Qu'est-ce que vous faites ensemble?
a On fait tout ensemble parce qu'on aime les mêmes choses.
b On va à la SPA et on fait du shopping.

8 Pourquoi êtes-vous ami(e)s?
a On s'entend très bien et j'ai confiance en elle.
b On n'est pas différentes et on ne se dispute jamais.

 WRITING 2 À toi de répondre aux questions!

1 Écoute!

Listen and list the activities in the order you hear them mentioned.

Exemple *1 = c*

2 Lis!

Read and say whether these statements are true or false. Explain in English.

Exemple **a** *false, because they're never together at school.*

a Magali et Isa are always together.
b Magali goes shopping without Isa.
c Magali and Isa don't have the same taste.

d They never quarrel.
e Magali often gives Isa presents.
f Magali knows she can trust Isa.

> Magali: «Je suis toujours avec Isa au collège. Je vais chez elle tous les jours. Je ne vais pas souvent faire du shopping sans elle. On n'aime pas toujours les mêmes choses, mais je ne me dispute jamais avec elle. Je lui donne des petits cadeaux pour son anniversaire et à Noël. J'ai beaucoup confiance en elle. C'est ma meilleure copine.»

3 Parle!

Speak about your pocket money. Say the following:

- who gives it to you
- how often you get money

- how much you get
- what you buy with your pocket money

Exemple *Ma mère me donne 10 livres par mois.*
Elle me donne aussi de l'argent pour...
J'achète...

4 Écris!

Imagine you went to an international school party. Write a paragraph about what you did:

- what you ate
- what you drunk

- what activities you tried
- give your opinion

Exemple *Je suis allé(e) à la fête internationale de l'école la semaine dernière. J'ai mangé... J'ai essayé...*

Le temps libre	*Free time*
je vais au cinéma	*I go to the cinema*
j'écoute de la musique	*I listen to music*
je fais du shopping	*I go shopping*
je fais du sport	*I do sport*
je joue à des jeux vidéo	*I play video games*
je regarde la télévision	*I watch television*
je sors avec des copains / copines	*I go out with friends*
je vais sur Internet	*I go on the Internet*

L'argent de poche	*Pocket money*
Ma mère me donne de l'argent de poche.	*My mother gives me pocket money.*
Mon père me donne 10 euros...	*My father gives me 10 euros...*
par semaine	*per week*
par mois	*per month*
pour mon anniversaire	*for my birthday*
pour Noël	*for Christmas*
je travaille	*I work*

Qu'est-ce que tu achètes?	*What do you buy?*
des places de cinéma	*cinema tickets*
des bonbons	*sweets*
des accessoires de mode	*fashion accessories*
des livres	*books*
des affaires d'école	*school stationery*
des CD / DVD / MP3	*CDs / DVDs / MP3s*
des magazines	*magazines*
des places de cinéma / de concert	*cinema / concert tickets*
des vêtements	*clothes*
J'ai acheté un CD.	*I bought a CD.*
Je vais acheter un CD.	*I will buy a CD.*

Quand	*When*
hier	*yesterday*
la semaine dernière	*last week*
le mois dernier	*last month*
demain	*tomorrow*
la semaine prochaine	*next week*
le mois prochain	*next month*

Mes copains	*My friends*
mon meilleur copain / ma meilleure copine	*my best friend*
avec lui / elle	*with him / her*
sans lui / elle	*without him / her*
chez lui / elle	*at his / her place*
pour lui / elle	*for him / her*
les mêmes choses que lui / qu'elle	*the same things as him / her*
J'ai confiance en lui / elle.	*I trust him / her.*
Je me dispute avec...	*I quarrel with...*

Une mégafête	*A big event*
un projet	*a proposal*
une équipe	*a team*
avant	*before*
après	*after*
une affiche	*a poster*
fabriquer	*to make*
un drapeau	*a flag*
un pays	*a country*
ranger	*to tidy up*
j'ai essayé	*I tried*
c'était	*it was*
J'ai bien aimé.	*I liked it.*
Je n'ai pas vraiment aimé.	*I didn't really like that.*

Fréquence	Frequency
toujours	*always*
tous les mois	*every month*
souvent	*often*
très souvent	*very often*
jamais	*never*
le matin	*in the morning*
l'après-midi	*in the afternoon*
le soir	*in the evening*
le dimanche	*on Sunday(s)*

À toi!

Look at the picture. Use words from the vocabulary list to imagine what these people are saying.

Le rock du samedi

Aujourd'hui, c'est samedi.
Je m'ennuie, oui, je m'ennuie*. *I'm bored
Je n'ai rien, rien à faire.
Rien rien... rien à faire!

Dring, dring, dring, dring
C'est Sylvain au téléphone.
Il veut faire les magasins,
aller manger vietnamien.
D'accord Sylvain, attends-moi,
J'arrive! Ehhhh... me voilà!

Dring, dring, dring, dring
C'est Anya au téléphone.
Elle m'invite au cinéma,
à jouer à la PS3.
D'accord Anya, attends-moi,
J'arrive! Ehhhh... me voilà!

Dring, dring, dring, dring
C'est Kévin au téléphone.
C'est la fête chez sa copine.
On danse le zouk,
 la biguine*. *West Indian dances
D'accord Kévin, attends-moi,
J'arrive! Ehhhh... me voilà!

Aujourd'hui, c'est samedi.
Je m'amuse bien,
 je m'amuse bien*. *I'm having fun
Les copains, oui, c'est super.
C'est, c'est, c'est... super bien!

1 Lis et écoute. Numérote les photos dans l'ordre de la chanson!

2 *READING* Trouve:
• I have nothing to do • Wait for me • Here I am

3 *SPEAKING* À deux: inventez d'autres couplets.
Exemple *Dring, dring, dring, dring.*
C'est Annette au téléphone.
Elle veut jouer au basket,
et aller sur Internet. Etc.

4 Chante avec le CD!

Read the story and find:
- 3 ways of attracting someone's attention politely
- 4 ways of asking for a bank

Invent another frame to go before frame 5.

Example Robber: *Pour aller à la banque, s'il vous plaît?*
Passer-by: *Oh, prenez le bus.*

Défi!

Invent a different ending for the cartoon.

À table, en France: On doit... ou on ne doit pas...?

1 mettre les coudes sur la table
2 mettre les mains sur la table
3 mettre les mains sous la table

7 couper le pain avec les mains
8 mettre le pain sur la table
9 nettoyer l'assiette avec le pain

4 prendre la fourchette avec la main gauche et le couteau avec la main droite
5 mettre le couteau dans la bouche
6 mettre la serviette autour du cou

10 manger les frites avec une fourchette
11 manger les frites avec les doigts
12 manger des fruits avec un couteau et une fourchette

On doit: 2, 4, 7, 8, 10, 12. On ne doit pas: 1, 3, 5, 6, 9, 11

 1a Read and look up new words in the dictionary. See page 21.

Example *la serviette = napkin (not towel)*

 1b List points 1–12 under one of these headings:

Example on doit	on ne doit pas
2	1

Défi!

Write a mini-guide to good table manners for your partner class in France.

Example *En Angleterre, on ne doit pas mettre le pain sur la table.*

BD = la bande dessinée = cartoon strip

Tu connais les héros de BD? Fais ce jeu-test. Choisis a ou b.

Astérix: il est petit avec un grand nez et une grande moustache blonde.

a Il est Gaulois. Il a un ami qui s'applle Obélix. Il a aussi un chien qui s'appelle Idéfix.

b Il est Gaulois. Il a quitté son village. Il est allé à Rome chez des amis romains.

Lucky Luke, le cowboy solitaire, est mince et brun.

a C'est un bandit. Il a tué des gens dans le désert.

b C'est un cowboy. Il a chassé les bandits et aidé les pauvres*.

*poor people

Tintin est un jeune journaliste. Il a les cheveux roux.

a Il a voyagé dans le monde entier avec son petit chien blanc Milou.

b Il a fait des enquêtes dans son village avec son grand chien noir Fifi.

1 **Read and find the French for:**

a he left   **d** he helped
b he travelled   **e** he chased
c he killed   **f** he made investigations

2 **Choose the character you like best and translate the information about them into English.**

Défi!

Invent a cartoon character and describe him/her.

Réponses: 1a, 2b, 3a, 4b

Marie-Antoinette a été la reine de France avant la Révolution française.

En 1773, Marie-Antoinette (14 ans) a épousé le roi de France.

Elle a dépensé beaucoup d'argent.

Elle a toujours bien mangé.

Elle a beaucoup chanté et elle a beaucoup dansé.

Mais en juillet 1789, les pauvres ont commencé la Révolution française!

Les Français ont attaqué les riches.

Ils ont mis Marie-Antoinette en prison.

Ils ont guillotiné Marie-Antoinette en 1793.

En 2006, on a fait un film sur Marie-Antoinette: l'actrice Kirsten Dunst a joué le rôle de Marie-Antoinette.

1 True or false?

a Marie-Antoinette was married to King Louis XVI.
b She was French.
c She had a rich and easy life.
d She was put in prison because she was rich.
e Marie-Antoinette was sent to the guillotine during the French Revolution.

2 Describe the appearance of Marie-Antoinette as played by Kirsten Dunst.

Moi, j'ai adoré Disneyland. Je suis arrivée très tôt le matin et je suis restée toute la journée. J'ai fait toutes les attractions. C'était sensationnel!

Ma sortie préférée, c'est quand je suis allée à un festival de musique à Reading. Ma grande sœur est venue avec moi. C'était génial.

L'année dernière, je suis allé en France avec mon père. On a vu un match de foot au Stade de France à Paris. Ma mère n'est pas venue parce qu'elle n'aime pas le football. C'était inoubliable!

Morgane, France

Amy, Angleterre

Je suis allé à la Cité de l'Espace à Toulouse en France. C'était très intéressant. J'ai vu une reproduction de la fusée Ariane 5 et j'ai fait une visite virtuelle de la Station spatiale internationale.

Victor, Belgique

Stefan, Allemagne

READING

1 **Who went to...?**

a a science park c a sports event
b a music event d a theme park

READING

2 **Read and find the French for:**

a my favourite outing d the atmosphere was great
b very early in the morning e Space City
c it was unforgettable f the Ariane 5 rocket

READING

3 **Which outing would you prefer? Explain why.**

Example *Je préfère la sortie au... parce que...*

Défi!

Write a speech bubble about the best outing of your life.

1 En 1961, pour la première fois, un homme est allé dans l'espace. Il a fait le tour de la Terre. C'était qui?
   a **Neil Armstrong**
   b **Youri Gagarine**

2 1965, c'est une année importante dans l'histoire de l'espace. Pourquoi?
   a **Un homme a flotté dans l'espace pour la première fois.**
   b **Un bébé est né dans l'espace.**

3 Le 21 juillet 1969, le premier astronaute a marché sur la Lune. C'était qui?
   a **Michael Collins**
   b **Neil Armstrong**

4 En 2001, l'Américain Dennis Tito était le premier touriste de l'espace. Il est allé dans la Station spatiale internationale. C'était combien?
   a **5 000 euros**
   b **Plus de 14 millions d'euros**

 1 **Read and find the French for:**

   a a man went into space
   b the first baby was born
   c the first astronaut walked on the moon
   d the first space tourist

 2 **In pairs, take turns to read a question aloud and answer.**

Réponses: 1b, 2a, 3b, 4b

De jeunes collégiens français ont écrit des poèmes sur quand ils étaient petits.

Quand j'étais petit, j'étais Samouraï.
Quand j'étais petit, je n'étais pas peureux.
Quand j'étais petit, c'était le temps des Jedi.
Quand j'étais petit, ce n'était pas ennuyeux!

Étienne

Quand j'étais petit, j'étais innocent.
Quand j'étais petit, je n'étais pas méchant.
Quand j'étais petit, c'était la guerre,
Quand j'étais petit, ce n'était pas super!

Haris

Quand j'étais petite, j'étais astronaute.
Quand j'étais petite, je n'étais pas sur terre.
Quand j'étais petite, c'était super!
Quand j'étais petite, ce n'était pas ma faute!

Marine

READING
1a Read the poems. Look up words you don't know in a bilingual dictionary.

SPEAKING
1b Who enjoyed their childhood? Who didn't? Explain why in English.

SPEAKING
2 Which poem do you prefer? Why?

Airness, c'est une marque de sport française. Les jeunes Français l'adorent!

Airness équipe* des clubs de football, de basket et d'athlétisme. Airness, c'est des vêtements, T-shirts, sweats, blousons, casquettes, chaussettes, chaussures! C'est aussi des accessoires: portables, lunettes, sacs, cahiers, trousses et stylos.

*equips

Le créateur d'Airness, c'est Malamine Koné. Il est très bon en boxe. Il devient champion de France amateur. Mais, en 1995, il a un accident de la route. Pour lui, la boxe, c'est fini. En 1999, il crée sa marque de sport. C'est un succès immédiat!

Pourquoi Airness?
C'est le surnom* du basketteur Michael Jordan, une idole de Koné.

nickname

Pourquoi la panthère?
'La Panthère', c'était le surnom de Koné quand il était boxeur.

1 **Read the article and find:**

a four sports　　**b** six items of clothing　　**c** six accessories

2 **Answer in English.**

a Who is the founder of Airness?
b Why didn't he become a professional boxer?
c When did he launch his brand?
d Why is the panther Airness's symbol?

Découvrez le programme des vacances d'été (7 juillet–29 août)

Du lundi au vendredi, de 9 h 30 à 17 h.
Le repas est compris.

Le programme

ATHLÉTISME, avec le Stade Français (8–16 ans)

BADMINTON (9–16 ans)

BASKET, avec le Paris Basket 18 (9–16 ans)

BOXE (9–16 ans)

CAPOEIRA – HIP-HOP (9–16 ans)

ÉCHECS, avec la Ligue Île de France d'Échecs (9–16 ans)

ESCALADE – TRAMPOLINE (10–16 ans)

FOOTBALL (10–16 ans)

GOLF, avec le Racing Club de France (10–13 ans)

HANDISPORTS, avec le Comité Régional Île de France Handisports (tous âges)

NATATION (10–16 ans)

ROLLER (8–16 ans)

ROLLER – BEACH-VOLLEY (8–16 ans)

RUGBY A 7, avec le PUC rugby (11–16 ans)

TENNIS (10–16 ans), avec le Paris Racing Lagardère et l'ASPAP

TENNIS DE TABLE (10–16 ans)

TIR À L'ARC – ESCRIME (10–16 ans)

VOILE ET KAYAK (10–16 ans)

 1 Read and answer these teenagers' queries:

a I'm 13. Can I learn boxing?
b Are there any water sports?
c How old do you need to be for the swimming?
d What is the athletics club called?
e How do you know there are no sessions at the weekend?

 2 Suggest one or two courses for Jean-Baptiste.

Jean-Baptiste: J'aime les sports d'équipe mais je n'aime pas l'eau. Je préfère rester à l'intérieur. J'aime bien la danse.

 3 Which courses would you prefer? Look up the names of any you don't know. Then, list your top five in order of preference.

Défi!

Write a short article in English for British pupils going to Paris explaining what summer activities are available in Paris.

C'est l'hiver. Il fait froid. Il neige. Il gèle. Les Français partent aux sports d'hiver!

Quand il y a du vent, on fait du snowkite. Ça se pratique avec un snowboard ou des skis. Avec le snowkite, ça va super vite!

Margaux:

J'adore aller à la montagne. La neige, c'est super. Je me réveille très tôt tous les jours. Je mets des vêtements chauds et je n'ai jamais froid. Souvent, il fait beau et il y a du soleil. Mon sport préféré, c'est le scooter des neiges (on dit aussi le snowscoot). C'est comme un scooter mais sur la neige!

Nico:

Je vais en classe de neige avec mon collège en février. On va à Avoriaz, dans les Alpes. Je m'amuse beaucoup. Il fait toujours beau: il ne pleut jamais. Je fais du ski tous les matins. L'année prochaine, je vais essayer le snow kayak. C'est comme le kayak mais sur la neige. Cool!

 1 Read and find the French for:

a it's cold   e it's fine
b it's snowing   f it's sunny
c it's icy   g it never rains
d it's windy

 2 Write six questions based on the article and swap with a partner. First read page 93 to help you.

Example *Qui va faire du snow kayak?*

 3 Write what activities you do in different weather.

Example *Quand il pleut, je regarde le foot à la télé.*

C'est quoi, une fête d'anniversaire réussie?

Alicia:
Le week-end dernier, je suis allée à la fête d'anniversaire de Sandrine. C'était génial! On a mangé des spaghetti bolognaise et un super gâteau au chocolat. On a discuté, on a écouté de la musique, on a joué au Monopoly et on a regardé des DVD. C'était sympa!

Pierre:
La semaine prochaine, on va fêter mes 13 ans et je vais inviter tous mes amis. Je vais jouer différentes musiques (sixties, rock, techno) et on va danser! On va manger des pizzas et des gâteaux. Ça va être très sympa!

Mathieu:
Je suis allé à une super fête pour les 15 ans de mon cousin. C'était très sympa. On a joué au foot dans le jardin et le soir, et on a regardé des films d'action.
J'ai adoré! On a dormi dans sa maison: on a beaucoup parlé mais on n'a pas beaucoup dormi!

 Read and find:
last weekend; a girlie party; next week; we'll celebrate; I'll invite; we'll dress up; it will be cool; last month; we've celebrated; it was cool; I loved it; we had a sleepover; we didn't sleep much

 Read again. Which party do you prefer? Why?

Example *Je préfère la fête de Pierre parce que j'adore danser!*

La recette de l'amitié

Mehdi: Ma recette de l'amitié

100 grammes de fidélité, 100 grammes de franchise et un kilo d'aventure.
Mélanger. Mettre dans un plat.
Manger avec les copains!

Zoé: Ma recette de l'amitié

Tu prends un litre de bonne volonté et une boîte de sincérité. Tu ajoutes trois cuillers de responsabilité.
Tu mets dans un plat! Bon appétit!

Anna: Ma recette de l'amitié

D'abord, mets de la gentillesse. Ajoute de la confiance.
Mets un peu d'aventure. Mélange. Mange tous les jours!

1a **Read the recipes. Look up words you don't know in a bilingual dictionary.**

1b **Make a note of all the ingredients mentioned. Write them in order of importance for you.**

Grammaire

Introduction

Here is a summary of the main points of grammar covered in **Clic! 2**, with some activities to check that you have understood and can use the language accurately.

Glossary of terms

noun *un nom* = a person, animal, place or thing
  Max achète du **pain** au **supermarché**.

determiner *un déterminant* = goes before a noun to introduce it
  le chien, **un** chat, **du** jambon, **mon** frère

singular *le singulier* = one of something
  Le chien mange **un biscuit**.

plural *le pluriel* = more than one of something
  Les filles font du judo.

pronoun *un pronom* = a little word used instead of a noun or name
  Il mange un biscuit. **Elles** font du judo.

verb *un verbe* = a "doing" or "being" word
  Je **parle** anglais. Il **est** blond. On **va** à la piscine. Nous **faisons** de la natation.

adjective *un adjectif* = a word which describes a noun
  Ton frère est **sympa**.
  C'est un appartement **moderne**.

preposition *une préposition* = describes position: where something is
  Mon livre est **sur** la table. J'habite **à** Paris.

1 Nouns and determiners
les noms et les déterminants

1.1 Masculine or feminine?

All French nouns are either masculine or feminine. Words for 'the' or 'a' must match:

	masculine words	feminine words
a or *an*	un	une
the	le	la

For example: **un** *sport*, **le** *nez* = masculine
une *question*, **la** *tête* = feminine

Important! When you meet a new noun, learn whether it is masculine or feminine.

Learn	*une pomme*	✓
not	*pomme*	✗

1.2 Singular or plural?

Most French nouns add *-s* to make them plural, just as in English:

la jambe ➔ *les jambe***s**

In French, the *-s* at the end of the word is not usually pronounced.

Some nouns do not follow this regular pattern:
- nouns ending in *-s*, *-x* or *-z* usually stay the same:
  le bras ➔ *les bras*
  le nez ➔ *les nez*

In front of plural nouns, the determiners change:

un/une ➔ *des*   *le/la* ➔ *les*

*Nina mange **une** banane. Nina mange **des** bananes.*
***Le** professeur parle. **Les** professeurs parlent.*

1.3 de + noun

	singular	plural
masculine words	du (*or* de l')	des
feminine words	de la (*or* de l')	des

Use *du, de la, de l'* or *des* + noun to say *some* or *any*.

*On a mangé **des** frites.* We ate **some** chips.
*Tu as **du** chocolat?* Have you got **any** chocolate?

(For how to say *any* in a negative sentence, see section 7.2)

2 Adjectives
les adjectifs

2.1 Form of adjectives

In English, whatever you are describing, the adjective stays exactly the same. In French, the adjective changes to match the word it is describing. Like the noun, it must be either masculine or feminine, singular or plural.

To show this, there are special adjective endings:

For example:
mon père est petit   *mes frères sont petit***s**
*ma mère est petit**e***   *mes sœurs sont petit**es***

Exceptions:

	singular	plural
masculine words	add nothing	add *-s*
feminine words	add *-e*	add *-es*

- Adjectives ending in *-s* don't add another in the masculine plural (but they do add *-es* in the feminine plural):
  un pantalon gris   *les cheveux gris*
  *les chaussettes gris**es***

Grammaire

Adjectives that end in *-e* don't add another in the feminine (but they do add *-s* when they describe plural words):

un frère calme ➔ *une sœur calme*
*des enfants calme**s***

Some adjectives have their own pattern:

singular		plural	
masculine	**feminine**	**masc./mixed**	**feminine**
blanc	blanche	blancs	blanches
bon	bonne	bons	bonnes
gros	grosse	gros	grosses
violet	violette	violets	violettes
beau*	belle	beaux	belles
nouveau*	nouvelle	nouveaux	nouvelles
vieux*	vieille	vieux	vieilles

 A **Choose the correct adjective from each pair to fill in these sentences.**

1 J'habite dans une ✳✳✳ maison. | gros / vieille
2 Il a de ✳✳✳ yeux verts. | beaux / grosses
3 On a une ✳✳✳ prof de français. | belles / nouvelle
4 Tu aimes ma nouvelle robe ✳✳✳ ? | violette / blanc
5 Il mange une très ✳✳✳ glace à la vanille! | grosse / bon
6 Mon grand-père est un très ✳✳✳ homme. | vieux / vieil

2.2 Position of adjectives

In English, **adjectives** always come before the <u>noun</u> they describe:
a **red** <u>sweatshirt</u>, a **modern** <u>house</u>, **nice** <u>friends</u>.

In French, **adjectives** usually come after the <u>noun</u>:
*un <u>sweat</u> **rouge**, une <u>maison</u> **moderne**, des <u>copains</u> **sympa***.

Some adjectives break this rule of position. The following come before the noun:

grand	*petit*	*gros*
nouveau	*jeune*	*vieux*
beau	*bon*	*mauvais*

*un **nouveau** jean*   *la **jeune** fille*   *de **bonnes** idées*

 B **Copy these sentences, adding the adjectives in brackets in the correct position.**

1 J'ai acheté trois cartes postales. [belles]
2 C'est un nouveau film. [intéressant]
3 J'ai deux nouvelles à te dire! [bonnes]
4 Il a une nouvelle copine. [française]
5 J'adore mon jean noir. [vieux]
6 Il a une voiture rouge. [petite]
7 Tu poses toujours des questions. [intelligentes]
8 Il met de vieilles chaussures. [démodées]

2.3 Demonstrative adjectives

Ce, cet, cette, ces can be used instead of un, une, des or le, la, les to say this / these or that / those.

Tu aimes *ce* livre?	Do you like **this** book?
Je ne connais pas *cette* fille.	I don't know **that** girl.
Je prends *ces* chaussures.	I'll take **these** shoes.

	masculine	feminine
singular	ce (cet*)	cette
plural	ces	ces

* cet is used before masculine singular nouns that begin with a vowel or a silent h (cet étage, cet hôtel)

3   The possessive
la possession

3.1 The possessive of nouns

Use noun + *de* + noun to show who (or what) things belong to:

*les baskets de **Joe***	**Joe's** trainers
*les questions **des élèves***	**the pupils'** questions

3.2 Possessive adjectives

These adjectives show who or what something belongs to (***my** bag*, ***your** CD*, ***his** brother*). They come before the noun they describe, in place of *un/une/des* or *le/la/les*, for example.

Like all adjectives, they match the noun they describe:

	singular		plural
	masculine	**feminine***	**masculine or feminine**
my	mon	ma	mes
your	ton	ta	tes
his/her	son	sa	ses

*Before a feminine noun that begins with a vowel, use *mon, ton, son* (*mon imagination, ton amie, son opinion*).

> ***Ma** sœur déteste **ton** frère.*
> **My** sister hates **your** brother.

> *Il parle avec **sa** grand-mère.*
> He is talking to **his** grandmother.

The words for *his* and *her* are the same (either *son, sa* or *ses*, depending on the word that follows).

> *Nina adore **son** chien.*   Nina loves **her** dog.
> *Max adore **son** chien.*   Max loves **his** dog.

C **Copy these sentences, changing "my" to its French equivalent.**

1   Laura adore [my] sœur.
2   Alex joue au foot avec [my] frère.
3   Tous les jours, je sors [my] chiens.
4   J'ai beaucoup de vêtements dans [my] armoire.

---

4   Prepositions
les prépositions

These describe position:

4.1 à

à combines with *le* or *les* in front of the noun to form a completely new word:

à + le → *au*   *à + les* → *aux*

singular		plural
masculine	**feminine**	**masculine or feminine**
au	à la	aux

- Time
  Use *à* to say *at* a time:
  *Le film commence **à** huit heures.*
  The film starts **at** eight o'clock.

- Places
  Use *à* to say *at*, *in* or *to* a place, combining it with the determiner before masculine or plural words:
  *J'habite **à** Paris.*
  I live **in** Paris.
  *Je vais **à la** gare.*
  I am going **to the** station.
  *Il est **au** cinéma.*
  He's **at the** cinema.

- Parts of the body that hurt
  Use *à* in front of the part of the body, combining it with the determiner before masculine or plural words:
  *J'ai mal **à la** tête.*   I've got a headache.
  *Max a mal **au** dos.*   Max has backache.
  *Tu as mal **aux** dents?* Have you got toothache?

Grammaire

4.2 en

- Places

  In French, most names of countries are feminine.
  To say *in* or *to* these countries, use the word *en*:

  *Vous allez **en** France?*   Are you going **to** France?
  *J'habite **en** Écosse.*   I live **in** Scotland.

  But: For masculine names of countries, use *au* (or *aux* if the country is plural):

  *Cardiff est **au** pays de Galles.*
  Cardiff is **in** Wales.
  *Elle va **aux** États-Unis.*
  She's going **to the** United States.

  en ville = in or to town

- Means of transport

  Use *en* + name of means of transport to say how you travel:

***en** train*	**by** train
***en** bus*	**by** bus
***en** voiture*	**by** car
***en** avion*	**by** plane

  But: For walking or a two-wheeled vehicle, use *à* + means of transport (without a determiner):

  *Il va **à** pied.*   He is walking.
  *Elle va **à** vélo.*   She is going **by** bike.
  *Nous allons **à** mobylette.*   We are going **by** moped.

5   Pronouns
les pronoms

A pronoun is used instead of a noun or name to avoid repetition.
Example: **My cat** is called Tigger. **He** sleeps in a box.

5.1 Subject pronouns

The subject of a verb tells you who or what is doing the action of the verb. It is usually a noun, but sometimes it is a pronoun. In English, we use the following subject pronouns:

I   you   he   she   it   we   they

I'm learning French. Are **you**?
Annie is learning Italian. **She** loves it.

The French subject pronouns are:

I	=	*je*	
		j'	in front of a vowel or a silent h: *j'aime/j'habite*
you	=	*tu*	to a child, a friend or a relative
		vous	to an adult you are not related to, or more than one person
he	=	*il*	for a boy or man
she	=	*elle*	for a girl or woman
it	=	*il*	if the noun it refers to is masculine
		elle	if the noun it refers to is feminine
we	=	*nous*	
		on	used more than *nous* in conversation

Use *on* when speaking or writing to friends.
Use *nous* when writing more "official" texts.

they	=	*ils*	for a masculine plural or for a mixed group (masculine + feminine)
		elles	for a feminine plural
		on	for people in general

- *On*

  On can mean *you, we, they* or *one*.
  It is followed by the form of the verb that follows *il* or *elle*:

  *Chez moi, **on parle** arabe.*   At home **we speak** Arabic.

6 Verbs
les verbes

Verbs describe what is happening. If you can put "to" in front of a word or "-ing" at the end, it is probably a verb.

listen – to listen ✓ = a verb
try – to try ✓ = a verb
desk – to desk ✗ = not a verb
happy – to happy ✗ = not a verb

6.1 The infinitive

Verbs take different forms:
I do the dishes every day. Alan **does** too, but you **don't**.

Not all verb forms are listed in a dictionary. For example, you won't find *does* or *don't*. You have to look up the infinitive, to **do**.

Infinitives in French are easy to recognise as they normally end with either *-er*, *-re* or *-ir*. For example: *regarder, prendre, choisir*.

6.2 The present tense

A verb in the present tense describes an action which is taking place now or takes place regularly.

There are two present tenses in English:
I **am eating** an apple (now)   I **eat** an apple (every day).

There is only one present tense in French:
*Je **mange** une pomme (maintenant).*
*Je **mange** une pomme (tous les jours).*

6.3 Present tense verb endings

To describe an action, you need a subject (the person or thing doing the action) and a verb.

The ending of the verb changes according to who the subject is:
You eat/She eat**s**   We speak/He speak**s**

Verb endings change in French too, for the same reason.

6.4 Regular verbs in the present tense

Most French verbs follow the same pattern. They have regular endings. Typical endings for verbs that end in *-er*, like *aimer*, in the present tense are:

j'	aim**e**	nous	aim**ons**
tu	aim**es**	vous	aim**ez**
il/elle/on	aim**e**	ils/elles	aim**ent**

Some other verbs which follow the same pattern are:

arriver	to arrive	*nager**	to swim
détester	to hate	*parler*	to speak
écouter	to listen	*ranger**	to tidy
jouer	to play	*regarder*	to watch
*manger**	to eat		

* but: *nous mangeons, nageons, rangeons*

Typical endings for verbs that end in *-ir*, like *choisir* (to choose), in the present tense are:

je	choisi**s**	nous	choisi**ssons**
tu	choisi**s**	vous	choisi**ssez**
il/elle/on	choisi**t**	ils/elles	choisi**ssent**

Verbs which follow the same pattern:
finir to finish   *remplir* to fill

Typical endings for verbs that end in *-re*, like *vendre* (to sell), in the present tense are:

je	vend**s**	nous	vend**ons**
tu	vend**s**	vous	vend**ez**
il/elle/on	vend	ils/elles	vend**ent**

Verbs which follow the same pattern:
attendre to wait   *répondre* to answer

D **Copy and complete the verbs.**

1 Moi, je ne regard✳✳✳ pas souvent la télé.

2 Tu fin✳✳✳ les cours à quelle heure?

3 Il écout✳✳✳ beaucoup de chansons de rap.

4 Elle rempl✳✳✳ la fiche d'inscription.

5 On attend✳✳✳ le bus.

6 Nous n'aim✳✳✳ pas la viande.

7 Vous nag✳✳✳ à la piscine ou à la mer?

8 Ils fin✳✳✳ l'entraînement sportif à quelle heure?

9 Elles détest✳✳✳ le foot!

10 Léo et Alice ne répond✳✳✳ pas aux emails.

Grammaire

6.5 Irregular verbs in the present tense

Some verbs do not follow this regular pattern. They are irregular verbs. Try to learn them by heart.

Infinitive	Present	English
avoir (*to have*)	j'ai tu as il/elle a on a nous avons vous avez ils/elles ont	*I have* *you have (to a friend, child or relative)* *he/she/it has* *we/they have* *we have* *you have (to an adult or group of people)* *they have*
être (*to be*)	je suis tu es il/elle est on est nous sommes vous êtes ils/elles sont	*I am* *you are (to a friend, child or relative)* *he/she/it is* *we/they are* *we are* *you are (to an adult or group of people)* *they are*
acheter (*to buy*)	j'achète tu achètes il/elle achète on achète nous achetons vous achetez ils/elles achètent	*I buy* *you buy (to a friend, child or relative)* *he/she/it buys* *we/they buy* *we buy* *you buy (to an adult or group of people)* *they buy*
aller (*to go*)	je vais tu vas il/elle va on va nous allons vous allez ils/elles vont	*I go* *you go (to a friend, child or relative)* *he/she/it goes* *we/they go* *we go* *you go (to an adult or group of people)* *they go*
boire (*to drink*)	je bois tu bois il/elle boit on boit nous buvons vous buvez ils/elles boivent	*I drink* *you drink (to a friend, child or relative)* *he/she/it drinks* *we/they drink* *we drink* *you drink (to an adult or group of people)* *they drink*

Infinitive	Present	English
devoir (*to have to/must*)	je dois	*I must*
	tu dois	*you must (to a friend, child or relative)*
	il/elle doit	*he/she/it must*
	on doit	*we/they must*
	nous devons	*we must*
	vous devez	*you must (to an adult or group of people)*
	ils/elles doivent	*they must*
faire (*to do/make*)	je fais	*I make/do*
	tu fais	*you make/do (to a friend, child or relative)*
	il/elle fait	*he/she/it makes/does*
	on fait	*we/they make/do*
	nous faisons	*we make/do*
	vous faites	*you make/do (to an adult or group of people)*
	ils/elles font	*they make/do*
se lever (*to get up*)	je me lève	*I get up*
	tu te lèves	*you get up (to a friend, child or relative)*
	il/elle se lève	*he/she/it gets up*
	on se lève	*we/they get up*
	nous nous levons	*we get up*
	vous vous levez	*you get up (to an adult or group of people)*
	ils/elles se lèvent	*they get up*
mettre (*to put on/wear*)	je mets	*I put (on)*
	tu mets	*you put (on) (to a friend, child or relative)*
	il/elle met	*he/she/it puts (on)*
	on met	*we/they put (on)*
	nous mettons	*we put (on)*
	vous mettez	*you put (on) (to an adult or group of people)*
	ils/elles mettent	*they put (on)*
pouvoir (*to be able to/can*)	je peux	*I can*
	tu peux	*you can (to a friend, child or relative)*
	il/elle peut	*he/she/it can*
	on peut	*we/they can*
	nous pouvons	*we can*
	vous pouvez	*you can (to an adult or group of people)*
	ils/elles peuvent	*they can*
préférer (*to prefer*)	je préfère	*I prefer*
	tu préfères	*you prefer (to a friend, child or relative)*
	il/elle préfère	*he/she/it prefers*
	on préfère	*we/they prefer*
	nous préférons	*we prefer*
	vous préférez	*you prefer (to an adult or group of people)*
	ils/elles préfèrent	*they prefer*

Grammaire

Infinitive	Present	English
prendre (*to take*)	je prends	*I take*
	tu prends	*you take (to a friend, child or relative)*
	il/elle prend	*he/she/it takes*
	on prend	*we/they take*
	nous prenons	*we take*
	vous prenez	*you take (to an adult or group of people)*
	ils/elles prennent	*they take*
venir (*to come*)	je viens	*I come*
	tu viens	*you come (to a friend, child or relative)*
	il/elle vient	*he/she/it comes*
	on vient	*we/they come*
	nous venons	*we come*
	vous venez	*you come (to an adult or group of people)*
	ils/elles viennent	*they come*
vouloir (*to want*)	je veux	*I want*
	tu veux	*you want (to a friend, child or relative)*
	il/elle veut	*he/she/it wants*
	on veut	*we/they want*
	nous voulons	*we want*
	vous voulez	*you want (to an adult or group of people)*
	ils/elles veulent	*they want*

 E Copy the sentences with the correct form of the verb.

1 Tu **viens** / **vient** avec moi?

2 Nous **prenons** / **prend** le bus à huit heures.

3 Ils **devons** / **doivent** travailler plus.

4 Qu'est-ce que vous **faites** / **font** le week-end?

5 Tu **veux** / **voulez** aller au cinéma samedi soir?

6 On ne **peut** / **pouvons** pas sortir samedi.

7 Je **vas** / **vais** chez ma copine Alice.

8 Les parents d'Alice **ont** / **a** une belle maison!

9 Mon frère **sort** / **sors** souvent le week-end.

10 Mes copains ne **sommes** / **sont** pas là pendant les vacances.

6.6 The perfect tense

A verb in the perfect tense (*passé composé*) describes an action which happened in the past. There are several ways to translate the *passé composé* in English:

> **J'ai regardé** la télé.
> **I watched** TV or **I have watched** TV.

For the *passé composé*, you need two parts: the present tense of *avoir* or *être* + the past participle of the main verb. See 6.7, 6.8, 6.9.

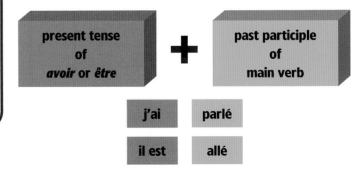

6.7 The past participle

To form the past participle, take the infinitive of the verb and change the ending:

- infinitives ending in *-er*: past participle ends in *-é*
  manger → *mangé*   *parler* → *parlé*
- infinitives ending in *-ir*: past participle ends in *-i*
  choisir → *choisi*   *sortir* → *sorti*
- infinitives ending in *-re*: past participle ends in *-u*
  descendre → *descendu*   *vendre* → *vendu*

Learn by heart these exceptions to the rule:

avoir → **eu**   *être* → **été**   *écrire* → **écrit**

faire → **fait**   *voir* → **vu**   *boire* → **bu**

lire → **lu**   *venir* → **venu**   *mettre* → **mis**

prendre → **pris** *pouvoir* → **pu**

devoir → **dû**   *vouloir* → **voulu**

F **Read this account of a party and note all 12 past participles used.**

La semaine dernière, j'ai organisé une boum pour mes 13 ans. J'ai écrit des invitations: 20 copains ont répondu. Mon correspondant français aussi est venu! Ma mère a fait un énorme gâteau. On a mis des costumes, on a dansé et on a bu du punch sans alcool. J'ai eu beaucoup de cadeaux, et mon père a pris des photos. La fête a fini à minuit. Tout le monde a été très content.

6.8 avoir + past participle

Most verbs form the perfect tense with part of *avoir*:

present	passé composé		
		avoir	past participle
je regarde	j'	ai	regardé
tu regardes	tu	as	regardé
il regarde	il	a	regardé
elle regarde	elle	a	regardé
on regarde	on	a	regardé
nous regardons	nous	avons	regardé
vous regardez	vous	avez	regardé
ils regardent	ils	ont	regardé
elles regardent	elles	ont	regardé

G **Copy this account of a healthy day. Replace the verbs (in brackets) with the correct form of the past participle.**

Aujourd'hui, pour être en forme, j'ai [manger] des fruits au petit déjeuner et j'ai [boire] du lait. Après, j'ai [faire] un peu d'exercice: je n'ai pas [prendre] le bus mais j'ai [marcher] 30 minutes pour aller au collège. À la cantine, je n'ai pas [choisir] les frites mais la salade. Le soir, après l'école, j'ai [jouer] au basket. À 22 heures, j'ai [dormi]!

6.9 être + past participle

Some verbs form their *passé composé* with *être*, not *avoir*. They are mostly verbs that indicate movement. You will need to learn by heart which they are.

Try learning them in pairs:

arriver / partir	to arrive / to leave
aller / venir	to go / to come
entrer / sortir	to go in / to go out
monter / descendre	to go up / to go down
rentrer / retourner	to go home / to go back to
tomber / rester	to fall / to stay
naître / mourir	to be born / to die

- The ending of the past participle changes when it comes after *être* in the *passé composé*. It agrees with the subject of the verb (masculine/feminine, singular/plural).

 *Je suis all**é** en France.*
*(Il est all**é** en France.)*

 *Je suis all**ée** en France.*
*(Elle est all**ée** en France.)*

 *Ils sont all**és** en France.*

*Elles sont all**ées** en France.*

For perfect tense with reflexive verbs, see 6.12.

Grammaire

 Copy these sentences, adding the ending -e, -s or -es to the past participle if needed.

1 Hier, ma sœur est allé∗∗∗ en vacances à Londres.

2 Nina et Sophie sont resté∗∗∗ à Paris.

3 Joe est venu∗∗∗ voir son correspondant Max.

4 Joe et Max sont allé∗∗∗ faire des courses.

5 Max et Nina sont sorti∗∗∗ à Bercy avec Joe.

6 Les parents de Joe sont venu∗∗∗ le chercher.

 Copy the sentences and add in the correct form of *avoir* or *être*.

1 Nina ∗∗∗ organisé une fête.

2 Max ∗∗∗ arrivé en retard.

3 Les invités ∗∗∗ mangé des gâteaux.

4 Max et Joe ∗∗∗ bu des sodas.

5 Les garçons ∗∗∗ partis vers 22 heures.

6 Les filles ∗∗∗ restées dormir chez Nina.

6.10 Reflexive verbs

Reflexive verbs need a pronoun between the subject and the verb.

subject	pronoun	verb	
Je	**me**	lève	(I get myself up) I get up.
Je	**m'**	habille	(I dress myself) I get dressed

Some common reflexive verbs: *se laver, se brosser les dents, se réveiller, s'amuser, s'ennuyer, se coucher, se reposer*

- The pronoun changes according to the subject it goes with:

je	+	**me / m'**	nous	+	**nous**
tu	+	**te / t'**	vous	+	**vous**
il / elle / on	+	**se / s'**	ils / elles	+	**se / s'**

6.11 Verb + infinitive

Sometimes there are two verbs next to each other in a sentence. In French, the form of **the first verb depends on the subject**, and the second verb is in the infinitive.

J'aime <u>aller</u> *au cinéma.*	I like going to the cinema.
Tu dois <u>faire</u> *tes devoirs.*	You must do your homework.
On préfère <u>lire</u> *ce livre.*	We prefer to read this book.
Il va <u>manger</u> *une pomme.*	He's going to eat an apple.

- *aller* + infinitive − talking about the future
  Use the present tense of the verb *aller* followed by an infinitive to talk about something that is going to happen in the near future:
  Je vais retrouver *Juliette à six heures.*
  I'm going to meet Juliette at six o'clock.
  Ils vont manger *au restaurant ce soir.*
  They are going to eat at the restaurant this evening.

- *devoir, pouvoir, vouloir*
  These verbs are nearly always followed by <u>the infinitive of another verb</u>.
  devoir − to have to (must)
  Elle doit <u>se coucher</u>   **She has to** go to bed.
  Vous devez <u>manger</u> *des légumes.* **You must** eat vegetables.

  pouvoir − to be able to (can)
  On peut <u>se retrouver</u> *demain?*   **Can we meet** tomorrow?
  Je peux <u>venir</u> *chez toi.*   **I can** come to your house.

  vouloir − to want
  Tu veux <u>rester</u> *à la maison?* **Do you want** to stay at home?
  Ils veulent <u>écouter</u> *des CD.* **They want** to listen to CDs.

See the full pattern of these verbs on pages 138−139.

 Copy and complete these sentences. Choose the correct form of each verb to go in front of the infinitive.

> aime aimez doit doivent
> allez peuvent veux préfère

1 J'*** beaucoup <u>aller</u> au cinéma.

2 Je *** <u>voir</u> le nouveau film de James Bond.

3 Nous, on *** <u>aller</u> au théâtre qu'au cinéma.

4 Vous *** <u>sortir</u> le soir?

5 Vous *** <u>sortir</u> demain soir?

6 Non, on *** <u>faire</u> nos devoirs. Beurk!

7 Elles *** <u>rester</u> à la fête jusqu'à 22 h.

8 Elles *** <u>aller</u> à la maison après 22 h.

6.12 jouer à / jouer de

To talk about playing games or sport, use *jouer **à***:

*J'aime jouer **au** football.*   I like playing football.

To talk about playing a musical instrument, use *jouer **de***:

*Je joue **de la** guitare.*   I play the guitar.

Remember:

à + le = **au**   de + le = **du**
à + les = **aux**   de + les = **des**

7 Negatives
la négation

In English, the negative form uses the word *not* or *-n't* as in *doesn't, don't, haven't, hasn't.*

In French, use **ne** ... **pas** around the verb (*ne* = *n'* in front of a vowel or a silent *h*):

*Je **ne** suis **pas** français.*   I'm **not** French.
*Elle **n'**a **pas** de sandales.*   She has**n't** got any sandals.
*On **ne** regarde **pas** la télé.*   We do**n't** watch TV.

7.1 ne ... jamais, ne ... plus

There are other negatives which also go around the verb:

ne (or *n'*) ... *jamais*   never
ne (or *n'*) ... *plus*   no longer, no more

*Je **ne** vais **jamais** au cinéma.*
I **never** go to the cinema.
*Il **n'**habite **plus** en France.*
He **no longer** lives in France.

8 Asking questions

- You can ask questions by making your voice go up at the end:
  Tu aimes le fromage.   *Tu aimes le fromage?*
  You like cheese.   Do you like cheese?

- You can start with *est-ce que* ...:
  Est-ce qu'il y a un bon film?
  Is there a good film on?

- You can use question words:
  - **combien**
    Ça fait combien?   How much is it?
    Tu es resté combien de temps?   How long did you stay?
  - **comment**
    C'était comment?   What was it like?
  - **où**
    Tu es allé où?   Where did you go?
  - **pourquoi**
    Tu n'es pas venu. Pourquoi?   You didn't come. Why?
  - **qu'est-ce que**
    Qu'est-ce que tu as fait?   What did you do?
  - **quand**
    Tu es parti quand?   When did you leave?
  - **quel/quelle/quels/quelles**
    Tu as quel âge?   How old are you?
    Il est quelle heure?   What time is it?
  - **qui**
    C'est qui?   Who is it?
    Qui aime le rap?   Who likes rap?
  - **quoi**
    C'est quoi, ton style préféré? What style do you prefer?

Grammaire

K **Match the questions and the answers.**

1 Tu es parti. Pourquoi?

2 Tu es parti où?

3 Tu es parti quand?

4 Tu es parti comment?

5 Tu es parti avec qui?

6 Tu es parti combien de temps?

7 Qu'est-ce que tu as mangé?

8 C'était comment?

a Un an.

b En avion.

c Délicieux!

d Le 1er janvier.

e Du serpent et du crocodile.

f Avec un copain.

g En Asie et en Australie.

h Pour explorer le monde.

Answers to grammar activities

A **1** vieille, **2** beaux, **3** nouvelle, **4** violette, **5** grosse, **6** vieil

B
1 belles cartes postales
2 un nouveau film intéressant
3 deux bonnes nouvelles
4 une nouvelle copine française
5 mon vieux jean noir
6 une petite voiture rouge
7 des questions intelligentes
8 de vieilles chaussures démodées

C **1** ma **2** mon **3** mes **4** mon

D **1** e, **2** is, **3** e, **4** it, **5** –, **6** ons, **7** ez, **8** issent, **9** ent, **10** ent

E **1** viens **2** prenons **3** doivent **4** faites **5** veux
6 peut **7** vais **8** ont **9** sort **10** sont

F organisé, écrit, répondu, venu, fait, mis, dansé, bu, eu,
pris, fini, été

G j'ai mangé, j'ai bu, j'ai fait, j'ai pris, j'ai marché, je n'ai pas
choisi, j'ai joué, j'ai dormi

H **1** allée **2** restées **3** venu **4** allés **5** sortis
6 venus

I **1** a **2** est **3** ont **4** ont **5** sont **6** sont

J **1** aime **2** veux **3** préfère **4** aimez **5** allez
6 doit **7** peuvent **8** doivent

K **1** h **2** g **3** d **4** b **5** f **6** a **7** e **8** c

Expressions utiles

Greetings	
Hello	*Bonjour*
	Salut (to a friend)
Hello (after about 6.00 pm)	*Bonsoir*
Good night (when going to bed)	*Bonne nuit*
Goodbye	*Au revoir*
	Salut (to a friend)

The French tend to use *monsieur / madame* in greetings:
Bonjour, monsieur. (e.g. to a shopkeeper)
Bonjour, madame.

Linking words	
Linking words join phrases and sentences together.	
also	*aussi*
like	*comme*
and	*et*
but	*mais*
or	*ou*
because	*parce que, car*
when	*quand*
on the other hand	*par contre*
then	*puis / ensuite*
in addition, also	*en plus*

Grammaire

Quantities — *les quantités*

See grammar section 1.3 for how to say *some* and *any*.

noun + *de/d'*

a bottle of (lemonade)	*une bouteille de (limonade)*
a litre of (mineral water)	*un litre d'(eau minérale)*
a glass of (milk)	*un verre de (lait)*
a packet of (sweets)	*un paquet de (bonbons)*
a tin of (tuna)	*une boîte de (thon)*
a kilo of (carrots)	*un kilo de (carottes)*
100g of (cheese)	*100 grammes de (fromage)*
a slice of (ham)	*une tranche de (jambon)*
a slice/portion of (pizza)	*une part de (pizza)*

Days — *les jours de la semaine*

Monday	*lundi*
Tuesday	*mardi*
Wednesday	*mercredi*
Thursday	*jeudi*
Friday	*vendredi*
Saturday	*samedi*
Sunday	*dimanche*

Months — *les mois*

January	*janvier*
February	*février*
March	*mars*
April	*avril*
May	*mai*
June	*juin*
July	*juillet*
August	*août*
September	*septembre*
October	*octobre*
November	*novembre*
December	*décembre*

The time — *l'heure*

What time is it?	*Il est quelle heure?*
It is one o'clock.	*Il est une heure.*
What time is it at?	*C'est à quelle heure?*
It is at one o'clock.	*C'est à une heure.*

Il est ...

It's 7 pm (19.00).	*Il est dix-neuf heures.*
It's 1.15 pm (13.15).	*Il est treize heures quinze.*
It's 10.30 pm (22.30).	*Il est vingt-deux heures trente.*
It's 3.45 pm (15.45).	*Il est quinze heures quarante-cinq.*

Countries — *les pays*

Australia	*l'Australie*
Belgium	*la Belgique*
Burkina Faso	*le Burkina Faso*
Canada	*le Canada*
England	*l'Angleterre*
France	*la France*
Germany	*l'Allemagne*
Great Britain	*la Grande-Bretagne*
Ireland	*l'Irlande*
Italy	*l'Italie*
Luxembourg	*le Luxembourg*
New Caledonia	*la Nouvelle-Calédonie*
Northern Ireland	*l'Irlande du nord*
Scotland	*l'Écosse*
Spain	*l'Espagne*
Switzerland	*la Suisse*
the United States	*les États-Unis*
Wales	*le pays de Galles*
the West Indies	*les Antilles*

Numbers — *les nombres*

0	zéro	27	vingt-sept
1	un	28	vingt-huit
2	deux	29	vingt-neuf
3	trois	30	trente
4	quatre	40	quarante
5	cinq	50	cinquante
6	six	60	soixante
7	sept	70	soixante-dix
8	huit	71	soixante et onze
9	neuf	72	soixante-douze
10	dix	73	soixante-treize
11	onze	74	soixante-quatorze
12	douze	75	soixante-quinze
13	treize	76	soixante-seize
14	quatorze	77	soixante-dix-sept
15	quinze	78	soixante-dix-huit
16	seize	79	soixante-dix-neuf
17	dix-sept	80	quatre-vingts
18	dix-huit	81	quatre-vingt-un
19	dix-neuf	82	quatre-vingt-deux,
20	vingt		...
21	vingt et un	90	quatre-vingt-dix
22	vingt-deux	91	quatre-vingt-onze,
23	vingt-trois		...
24	vingt-quatre	100	cent
25	vingt-cinq	1000	mille
26	vingt-six		

Clic s'amuse! answers

Unit 1

Ça veut dire quoi?   b
Proverbes   1 b; 2 c; 3 a
Casse-tête   à gauche (Vehicles drive on the right-hand side in France, so as we can't see the door of this bus, it must be going towards the left.)

Unit 2

Ça veut dire quoi?   c
Casse-tête   It reads the same backwards as it does forwards.

Unit 3

Ça veut dire quoi?   c
Casse-tête   Espagne, Portugal, Maroc

Unit 4

Ça veut dire quoi?   a
Casse-tête: Qui suis-je?   a candle (I was tall before being small)
Vive les couleurs!   a rose; b bleue; c noir; d verts; e noires

Unit 5

Ça veut dire quoi?   d
Casse-tête   d'origine japonaise – le judo, le karaté, l'aïkido
d'origine britannique – le football, le jogging, le hockey
d'origine espagnole – la corrida

Unit 6

Ça veut dire quoi?   a
Casse-tête international: Qui suis-je?   la lettre "a"
Proverbes   1 b; 2 c; 3 a

Glossaire

Key

nm masculine noun   *nf* feminine noun
pl plural *v* verb   *adj* adjective
pp past participle

* Adjectives marked with an asterisk do not have a
separate feminine form.

† Verbs marked with a dagger are formed with
être (*not avoir*) in the perfect tense.

A

il/elle/on **a** he/she has; we/you have
    – *from* **avoir**
à to
d' **abord** first
d' **accord** OK
être d' **accord** to agree
j' **achète** I buy – *from* **acheter**
acheter *v* to buy
un **acteur** *nm* an actor
une **actrice** *nf* an actress
une **adresse** *nf* an address
les **affaires** *nf pl* 1) clothes, stuff
    2) business
une **affiche** *nf* a poster
Tu as quel **âge?** How old are you?
j' **ai** I have – *from* **avoir**
j' **ai 15 ans** I'm 15 years old
aider *v* to help
aïe! ouch! oh dear!
l' **ail** *nm* garlic
ailleurs elsewhere
aimer *v* to like
j' **aimerais** (+ *infinitive*) I would like to...
ajouter *v* to add
allé gone *pp of* **aller**
l' **Allemagne** *nf* Germany
allemand/allemande *adj* German
aller *v* † to go
aller chercher *v* † to collect, to fetch
Allô! Hello! (*on the phone*)
une **allumette** *nf* a match
alors so
un/une **alpiniste** *nm/nf* a mountain climber
améliorer *v* to improve
amener *v* to take
américain/américaine *adj* American
l' **amitié** *nf* friendship
s' **amuser** *v* † to have fun
un **an** *nm* a year
un **ananas** *nm* a pineapple
anglais/anglaise *adj* English
un/une **Anglais/Anglaise** *nm/nf* an
    Englishman/Englishwoman
l' **Angleterre** *nf* England
un **animal** (*pl* **des animaux**) *nm*
    an animal
les **animations** *nf pl* activities

l' **année dernière** *nf* last year
l' **année prochaine** *nf* next year
les **années soixante** *nf pl* the 1960s
un **anniversaire** *nm* a birthday
août *nm* August
un **appartement** *nm* an apartment,
    a flat
s' **appeler** *v* † to be called
Je m' **appelle...** My name is...
apprendre *v* to learn
appris learned *pp of* **apprendre**
après after
l' **après-midi** *nm* (in the) afternoon
l' **arabe** *nm* Arabic
un **arbitre** *nm* a referee, an umpire
l' **argent** *nm* money
l' **argent de poche** *nm* pocket money
une **armoire** *nf* a wardrobe
un **arrêt de bus** *nm* a bus stop
arrêter *v* 1) to stop 2) to arrest
arriver *v* † to arrive
un **arrondissement** *nm* a district,
    borough (of Paris)
tu **as** you have – *from* **avoir**
un **ascenseur** *nm* a lift, an elevator
assez quite
une **assiette** *nf* a plate
un/une **athlète** *nm/nf* an athlete
l' **athlétisme** *nm* athletics
atteindre *v* to attain, to win
atteint attained, won *pp of* **atteindre**
attendre *v* to wait
attraper *v* to catch
au (+ *nm*) to the = à + le
Au revoir! Goodbye!
aujourd'hui today
l' **automne** *nm* autumn
autour de around
autre* *adj* other
aux (+ *npl*) to the = à + les
en **avance** in advance, early
avant before
avec with
vous **avez** you have –
    from **avoir**
un **avion** *nm* an aeroplane
un **avis** *nm* an opinion
à ton/votre **avis** in your opinion
avoir *v* to have
avril *nm* April

B

les **bagages** *nm pl* suitcases, luggage
une **bague** *nf* a ring
se **baigner** *v* † to swim in the sea
une **baleine** *nf* a whale
en **bande** in a group (*of friends*)
une **banque** *nf* a bank

un **bar-tabac** *nm* a bar which sells
    stamps and tobacco
en **bas** downstairs
le **basket** *nm* basketball
les **baskets** *nf pl* trainers
un **basketteur** *nm* a (*male*) basketball
    player
une **basketteuse** *nf* a (*female*) basketball
    player
une **bataille** *nf* a battle
un **bateau** (*pl* **des bateaux**) *nm* a boat
un **bâtiment** *nm* a building
battre *v* to beat
beau/bel/belle/beaux/belles *adj*
    beautiful, handsome
il fait **beau** the weather's fine
beaucoup de a lot of
un **bébé** *nm* a baby
belge* *adj* Belgian
la **Belgique** *nf* Belgium
belle *adj* – *see* **beau**
un/une **bénévole** *nm/nf* volunteer
avoir **besoin de** *v* to need
le **béton** *nm* concrete
le **beurre** *nm* butter
beurré/beurrée *adj* buttered
bien (+ *verb*) well
bien sûr of course
bientôt soon
À **bientôt!** See you soon!
Bienvenue! Welcome!
les **bijoux** *nm pl* jewellery
un **billet** *nm* a ticket
blanc/blanche *adj* white
bleu/bleue *adj* blue
blond/blonde *adj* blonde
un **blouson** *nm* a bomber-style jacket
boire *v* to drink
je/tu **bois** I/you drink – *from* **boire**
le **bois** *nm* wood
une **boisson** *nf* a drink
il/elle/on **boit** he/she drinks; we/you drink
    – *from* **boire**
une **boîte** *nf* a box, a can
une **boîte de nuit** *nf* a night club
bon/bonne *adj* good, right
Bon courage! Take heart!
bon marché* *adj* cheap
Bon voyage! Have a good trip!
un **bonbon** *nm* a sweet
le **bonheur** *nm* happiness
Bonjour! Hello!
bonne *adj* – *see* **bon**
de **bonne heure** early
Bonne nuit! Goodnight!
la **bonne volonté** *nf* goodwill
Bonsoir! Good evening!
au **bord de la mer** at/to the seaside
la **bouche** *nf* mouth

une **boucle d'oreille** (*pl* **des boucles d'oreilles**) *nf* earring
une **boulangerie** *nf* a baker's
un **boulevard** *nm* a boulevard (*wide, straight city street*)
un **boulot** *nm* a task, job
une **boum** *nf* a party
le **bout** *nm* end
une **bouteille** *nf* a bottle
une **boutique** *nf* a (small) shop
la **boxe** *nf* boxing
un **boxeur** *nm* a (*male*) boxer
une **boxeuse** *nm* a (*female*) boxer
le **bras** *nm* arm
un **brassard** *nm* a sweatband
la **Bretagne** *nf* Brittany
 breton/bretonne *adj* Breton
 britannique *adj* British
une **brosse à dents** *nf* a toothbrush
se **brosser les dents** *v* † to brush one's teeth
un **bruit** *nm* a noise
 brûlé/brûlée *adj* burnt
 brun/brune *adj* brown
 bu drunk *pp of* **boire**
une **bulle** *nf* a (speech) bubble

 Ça me plaît I like it
 Ça ne fait rien! It doesn't matter!
 Ça s'écrit comment? How do you write it? How do you spell it?
 Ça se prononce comment? How do you pronounce it?
 Ça va? How are you? (*to a friend*)
 Ça va I'm fine
une **cabine** *nf* a fitting room
 cacher *v* to hide
un **cadeau** (*pl* **des cadeaux**) *nm* a present
un **cahier** *nm* an exercise book
un **camion** *nm* a lorry
le **canoë** *nm* canoe, canoeing
une **capitale** *nf* a capital (city)
 car because
un **car** *nm* a coach (*transport*)
à **carreaux** checked
une **carte** *nf* 1) a card 2) a map 3) a menu
une **carte postale** *nf* a postcard
le **carton** *nm* cardboard
une **casquette** *nf* a (baseball) cap
 casser *v* to break
se **casser la jambe, le bras...** *v* † to break one's leg, arm...
un **cauchemar** *nm* a nightmare
 ce/cet/cette/ces this/these

 Ce n'est pas la peine! It's not worth it!
une **ceinture** *nf* a belt
 Cela m'est égal! I don't mind!
 célèbre *adj* famous
 cent one hundred
 cent deux one hundred and two
 cent un one hundred and one
un **centre-ville** *nm* a town or city centre
un **cerceau** (*pl* **des cerceaux**) *nm* a ring, hoop
une **cerise** *nf* a cherry
 c'est-à-dire that is, that's to say
 C'est par où? Which way is it?
une **chaîne** *nf* a (TV) channel
la **chaleur** *nf* heat
un **championnat** *nm* a championship
la **chance** *nf* luck
un **changement** *nm* a change
se **changer** *v* † to get changed
une **chanson** *nf* a song
 chanter *v* to sing
un **chanteur** *nm* a (*male*) singer
une **chanteuse** *nf* a (*female*) singer
un **chapeau** (*pl* **des chapeaux**) *nm* a hat
 chaque each
la **charcuterie** *nf* 1) a pork butcher's and delicatessen 2) cooked pork meats
 chasser *v* 1) to chase 2) to hunt
un **chat** *nm* a cat
un **château** (*pl* **des châteaux**) *nm* a castle, palace, chateau
se **chauffer** *v* † to keep warm
les **chaussettes** *nf pl* socks
les **chaussures** *nf pl* shoes
un **chef d'entreprise** *nm* a boss, director
le **chemin** (+ **pour** *or* **de**) *nm* the way (to)
une **chemise** *nf* a shirt
 cher/chère 1) expensive 2) dear (*beloved*)
un **cheval** (*pl* **des chevaux**) *nm* a horse
les **cheveux** *nm pl* hair
 chez Robert at Robert's (house)
un **chien** *nm* a dog
un **chiffre** *nm* a number (*digit*)
les **chips** *nf pl* crisps
 choisir *v* to choose
un **choix** *nm* a choice
le **ciel** *nm* sky
 cinq five
 cinquante fifty
 cinquante-deux fifty-two
 cinquante et un fifty-one
 cinquième *adj* fifth
en **cinquième** (*in France etc.*) = in Year 8

un **citron** *nm* a lemon
un **client** *nm* a (*male*) customer
une **cliente** *nf* a (*female*) customer
 cocher *v* to tick
le **cœur** *nm* heart
le **Colisée** *nm* the Coliseum (*a famous arena in Rome*)
 collectionner *v* to collect
un **collège** *nm* a secondary school (*11–15*)
un **collégien** *nm* a (secondary) schoolboy
une **collégienne** *nf* a (secondary) schoolgirl
un **collier** *nm* a necklace
 combien? how much?
 commander *v* to order (*e.g. in restaurant*) (*not 'to command'!*)
 comme like
 commencer *v* to start
 comment? how?
un **commissaire de police** *nm* a superintendent
 comprendre *v* to understand
 compris understood *pp of* **comprendre**
 compter *v* to count
un **concours** *nm* a competition
avoir **confiance** (+ **en**) to trust (someone)
 connaître *v* to know (*a person, place*)
 connu *pp of* **connaître**
la **conquête** *nf* conquest
un **conseil** *nm* a piece of advice
 conseiller *v* to advise
 construire *v* to construct
 construit built *pp of* **construire**
 content/contente *adj* happy, content
un **copain** *nm* a (*male*) friend
une **copine** *nf* a (*female*) friend
le **corps** *nm* body
un **correspondant** *nm* a (*male*) correspondent, penfriend
une **correspondante** *nm* a (*female*) correspondent, penfriend
 corriger *v* to correct
à **côté du/de la/des** next to
le **cou** *nm* neck
se **coucher** *v* † to go to bed
un **coucou** *nm* a cuckoo
le **coude** *nm* elbow
une **couleur** *nf* a colour
 coupable *adj* guilty
 couper *v* to cut
se **couper au genou, au doigt...** *v* † to cut one's knee, finger...

Glossaire

une **cour de récré(ation)** *nf* a playground
courir *v* to run
un **cours** *nm* a lesson, course
au **cours de** in the course of
court/courte *adj* short
un **cousin** *nm* a (*male*) cousin
une **cousine** *nf* a (*female*) cousin
un **couteau** *nm* a knife
une **cravate** *nf* a tie
créer *v* to create
un **cri** *nm* a shout
crier *v* to shout
croire *v* to believe
cru believed *pp of* **croire**
une **cuiller** *nf* a spoon
une **cuillerée** *nf* a spoonful
le **cuir** *nm* leather
faire **cuire** *v* to cook (*something*)
la **cuisine** *nf* 1) kitchen 2) cooking, cuisine

d'abord first
d'accord OK
le **Danemark** *nm* Denmark
dangereux/dangereuse *adj* dangerous
danois/danoise *adj* Danish
dans in
de from, of
décembre *nm* December
décevoir *v* to disappoint
découvrir *v* to discover
décrire *v* to describe
en **dehors de** outside of, other than
déjeuner *v* to have lunch
demain tomorrow
demander *v* to ask (*not* 'to demand'!)
déménager *v* to move house
dépenser *v* to spend
les **dépenses** *nf pl* expenditure
déplier *v* to unfold
depuis since, for (*time*)
dernier/dernière *adj* last
derrière behind
des 1) some 2) from the
= **de** + **les**
descendre *v* † to go down
désolé/désolée *adj* sorry
un **dessin** *nm* a drawing
dessiner *v* draw
détester *v* to dislike
deux two
à **deux** in a pair
deuxième* *adj* second
devant in front of

devenir *v* † to become
deviner *v* to guess
devoir *v* to have to, 'must'
les **devoirs** *nm pl* homework
un **dictionnaire** *nm* dictionary
dimanche *nm* (on) Sunday
dîner *v* to have dinner
dire *v* to say
un **directeur** *nm* a headmaster
une **directrice** *nf* a headmistress
je/tu **dis** I/you say – *from* **dire**
discuter *v* to discuss, to talk
se **disputer** (+ **avec**) *v* † to argue (with)
dit said *pp of* **dire**
dix ten
dix-huit eighteen
dix-neuf nineteen
dixième* *adj* tenth
un **doigt** *nm* a finger
je/tu **dois** I/you must
(c'est) **dommage!** it's a shame!
donner *v* to give
dormir *v* to sleep
le **dos** *nm* back
se **doucher** *v* † to have a shower
doux/douce *adj* sweet, gentle
douze twelve
un **drapeau** (*pl* **des drapeaux**) *nm* a flag
un **drogué** *nm* a (*male*) drug addict
une **droguée** *nf* a (*female*) drug addict
le **droit** *nm* law
(tout) **droit** straight on
à **droite** to the right
drôle* *adj* funny
dû had to *pp of* **devoir**
dur/dure *adj* hard
la **durée** *nf* length, duration

l' **eau** *nf* water
échanger *v* to exchange
une **écharpe** *nf* a scarf
les **échecs** *nm pl* chess
une **école** *nf* a school
une **école maternelle** *nf* an infant school
une **école primaire** *nf* a primary school
écolo(gique)* *adj* ecological
écossais/écossaise *adj* Scottish
l' **Écosse** *nf* Scotland
écouter *v* to listen
écrire *v* to write
écrit written *pp of* **écrire**
une **église** *nf* a church
un/une **élève** *nm/nf* a pupil
elle 1) she/it 2) her (*after prepositions such as* **après**, **chez** *etc. or for emphasis*)
elles 1) they 2) them (*f pl*) (*after*

prepositions such as **après**, **chez** *etc. or for emphasis*)
une **émission** *nf* a (television) programme
un **emploi** *nm* a job
en 1) in 2) some, any, of it
encore still; again
s' **endormir** *v* † to fall asleep
un **endroit** *nm* a place
l' **enfer** *nm* hell
s' **ennuyer** *v* † to be bored
ennuyeux/ennuyeuse *adj* boring
une **enquête** *nf* an enquiry
ensemble together
ensuite next, then
s' **entendre** (+ **avec**) *v* † to get on (with a person)
entier/entière *adj* whole, entire
l' **entraînement** *nm* training
s' **entraîner** *v* † to train
entre between
une **entrée** *nf* an entrance
une **entreprise** *nf* a firm (*business*)
entrer (+ **dans**) *v* † to enter, to go into
avoir **envie de** to want to
environ about
s' **envoler** (+ **vers**) *v* † to take off (for)
envoyer *v* to send
une **épaule** *nf* a shoulder
épouser *v* to marry
une **équipe** *nf* a team
les **équipements** *nm pl* equipment
équiper *v* to equip
l' **équitation** *nf* horse-riding
une **erreur** *nf* a mistake
tu **es** you are – *from* **être**
l' **escalade** *nf* climbing
l' **escrime** *nf* fencing
l' **espace** *nf* 1) space 2) (= *universe*) space
l' **Espagne** *nf* Spain
espagnol/espagnole *adj* Spanish
espérer *v* to hope
l' **espoir** *nm* hope
essayer *v* to try
il/elle/on **est** he/she is; we/you are – *from* **être**
l' **est** *nm* east
et and
un **étage** *nm* a floor, level
à l' **étage** upstairs
les **États-Unis** *nm pl* the United States
aux **États-Unis** in/to the United States
l' **été** *nm* summer
été been *pp of* **être**
vous **êtes** you are – *from* **être**
une **étoile** *nf* a star
étranger/étrangère *adj* foreign, strange
un/une **étranger/étrangère** *nm/nf* a

foreigner, stranger
être *v* to be
étudier *v* to study
eu had *pp of* **avoir**
eux them (*m pl*) (*after prepositions such as* **après**, **chez** *etc. or for emphasis*)
un **événement** *nm* an event
Je m' **excuse!** I'm sorry!
s' **excuser** *v* † to apologise
par **exemple** for example
expliquer *v* to explain
une **exposition** *nf* an exhibition

fabriquer *v* to make
en **face du/de la/des** opposite
facile* *adj* easy
une **façon** *nf* a way
j'ai **faim** I'm hungry
faire *v* to make, to do
faire (+ de) *v* to do (*a sport*)
fait made *pp of* **faire**
falloir *v* to be necessary
une **famille** *nf* a family
fatigué/fatiguée *adj* tired
il **faut +** *infinitive* it is necessary to
– *from* **falloir**
une **faute** *nf* a mistake
les **fautes d'orthographe** *nf pl* spelling mistakes
une **femme** *nf* 1) a woman 2) a wife
une **fenêtre** *nf* a window
fermer *v* to close
une **fête** *nf* a party
février *nm* February
une **fiche** *nf* a record sheet, form
fier/fière *adj* proud
une **fille** *nf* 1) a girl 2) a daughter
un **fils** *nm* a son
à la **fin de** at the end of
finir *v* to finish
une **fleur** *nf* a flower
flotter *v* to float
fluo* *adj* fluorescent
une **fois** *nf* a time, once
le **foot(ball)** *nm* football
une **forêt** *nf* a forest
la **forme** *nf* fitness, well-being
être en **forme** to be fit
fort/forte *adj* strong
fort loudly
une **fourchette** *nf* a fork
français/française *adj* French
en **français** in French
un **Français** *nm* a Frenchman
une **Française** *nf* a Frenchwoman

la **France** *nf* France
en **France** in/to France
la **franchise** *nf* sincerity
frapper *v* to hit, to strike
frisé/frisée *adj* frizzy, curly
les **frites** *nf pl* chips
froid/froide *adj* cold
avoir **froid** to be cold (*of a person*)
il fait **froid** it's cold (weather)
le **fromage** *nm* cheese
une **frontière** *nf* a border
fumer *v* to smoke
une **fusée** *nf* a rocket
fusiller *v* to shoot

gagner *v* to win, to earn
gallois/galloise *adj* Welsh
un **gant** *nm* a glove
un **garçon** *nm* a boy
Garçon! Waiter!
garder *v* to keep, to look after
garder la forme *v* to keep fit
une **gare** *nf* a railway station
un **gâteau** (*pl* **des gâteaux**) *nm* a cake
à **gauche** to the left
génial/géniale/géniaux/géniales *adj* great, brilliant
un **genou** (*pl* **les genoux**) *nm* a knee
les **gens** *nm pl* people
gentil/gentille *adj* nice
la **gentillesse** *nf* kindness
une **glace** *nf* 1) an ice cream 2) a mirror
un **glaçon** *nm* an ice cube
glisser *v* to slip, to slide
une **gomme** *nf* a rubber (*eraser*)
un **goût** *nm* a taste
goûter au/à la/aux *v* to taste, to try (*food*)
grand/grande *adj* big, tall
une **grand-mère** *nf* a grandmother
un **grand-père** *nm* a grandfather
la **Grande-Bretagne** *nf* Great Britain
les **grandes vacances** *nf pl* summer holidays
gratuit/gratuite *adj* free (*without cost*)
grave* *adj* serious
grec/grecque *adj* Greek
la **Grèce** *nf* Greece
gris/grise *adj* grey
gros/grosse *adj* fat
grossir *v* to get fat
une **guerre** *nf* a war
un **gymnase** *nm* a gymnasium

un **habitant** *nm* an inhabitant
J' **habite à...** I live in...
habiter *v* to live
d' **habitude** usually
une **héroïne** *nf* a heroine
un **héros** *nm* a hero
une **heure** *nf* an hour
à l' **heure** per hour
de bonne **heure** early
Quelle **heure est-il?** What time is it?
il est (une) **heure** it's (one) o'clock
à (sept) **heures** at (seven) o'clock
à (dix) **heures et demie** at half past (ten)
hier yesterday
hier soir yesterday evening
une **histoire** *nf* a story
l' **histoire** *nf* history
l' **hiver** *nm* winter
un **homme** *nm* a man
un **homme d'affaires** *nm* a businessman
un **hôpital** (*pl* **des hôpitaux**) *nm* a hospital
huit eight
huitième* *adj* eighth
humanitaire* *adj* humanitarian

une **idée** *nf* an idea
il he/it
il n'y a pas de/d'... there isn't/aren't any...
il y a un/une/des... there is/there are...
il y a (dix) ans (ten) years ago
une **île** *nf* an island
ils they (*m pl*)
un **immeuble** *nm* a block of flats
impoli/impolie *adj* impolite, rude
impressionnant/impressionnante *adj* impressive
l' **informatique** *nf* IT
inoubliable* *adj* unforgettable
s' **installer** *v* † to sit down, to settle into
intéressant/intéressante *adj* interesting
les **invités** *nm pl* guests
irlandais/irlandaise *adj* Irish
l' **Irlande** *nf* Ireland
l'**Italie** *nf* Italy
italien/italienne *adj* Italian

Glossaire

J

la **jalousie** *nf* jealousy
jamais never *see* **ne... jamais**
une **jambe** *nf* a leg
le **jambon** *nm* ham
janvier *nm* January
le **japonais** *nm* Japanese
un **jardin** *nm* a garden
jaune* *adj* yellow
je I
un **jeu** (*pl* **des jeux**) *nm* a game
un **jeu de société** (*pl* **des jeux**) *nm*
a board game
jeudi *nm* (on) Thursday
jeune* *adj* young
les **jeunes** *nm pl* young people
la **jeunesse** *nf* youth
jouer *v* (+ **à**) to play (*a sport*); (+ **de**)
to play (*an instrument*)
un **jouet** *nm* a toy
un **joueur** *nm* a (*male*) player
une **joueuse** *nf* a (*female*) player
un **jour** *nm* a day
un **jour férié** *nm* a bank holiday
un **journal** (*pl* **des journaux**) *nm* a
newspaper
une **journée** *nf* a day
la **journée scolaire** *nf* school day
juillet *nm* July
juin *nm* June
une **jupe** *nf* a skirt
le **jus** *nm* juice
jusqu'au/à la/aux... (all the way) to...
juste just

K

un **kiosque** *nm* a newspaper stand,
kiosk

L

la the (+ *nf*)
là there
un **lac** *nm* a lake
une **laisse** *nf* a (dog) lead
laisser *v* to leave (behind)
le **lait** *nm* milk
lancer *v* to throw
une **langue** *nf* 1) a tongue 2) a language
se **laver** *v* † to get washed
le **the** (+ *nm*)
les **légumes** *nm pl* vegetables
lent/lente *adj* slow
les **the** (+ *pl*)
leur/leurs their
lever *v* to lift
se **lever** *v* † to get up

libérer *v* to liberate
libre* *adj* free (*liberated*)
le **lieu de résidence** *nm* place of
residence
une **ligne** *nf* a line
lire *v* to read
un **lit** *nm* a bed
un **livre** *nm* a book
loin far
Londres London
long/longue *adj* long
longtemps a long time
lu read *pp of* **lire**
lui 1) to him, to her, to it 2) him (*after
prepositions such as* **après**, **chez**
etc. or for emphasis)
lundi *nm* (on) Monday
la **lune** *nf* the moon
les **lunettes** *nf pl* glasses (= *spectacles*)
les **lunettes de soleil** *nf pl* sunglasses

M

madame (*pl* **mesdames**) Madam
mademoiselle (*pl* **mesdemoiselles**)
Miss
un **magasin** *nm* a shop
un grand **magasin** *nm* a department store
un **magasin de sport** *nm* a sports shop
mai *nm* May
maigre* *adj* thin, skinny
un **maillot** *nm* a vest
la **main** *nf* hand
à la **main** by hand
maintenant now
se **maintenir en forme** *v* † to keep fit
la **mairie** *nf* town hall
mais but
une **maison** *nf* a house
mal bad(ly)
avoir **mal au dos, à la tête, à la gorge...**
to have backache, a headache, a
sore throat...
faire **mal** to hurt
malade* *adj* sick, ill
une **manche** *nf* a sleeve
manger *v* to eat
les **manières de table** *nf pl* table
manners
manquer *v* to be missing
un **manteau** (*pl* **des manteaux**) *nm* a
coat
le **maquillage** *nm* make-up
marcher *v* to walk
mardi *nm* (on) Tuesday
un **mari** *nm* a husband
se **marier** *v* † to get married
le **Maroc** *nm* Morocco
marocain/marocaine *adj* Moroccan

une **marque** *nf* a brand
marron* *adj* brown (*of eyes*)
mars *nm* March
un **match nul** *nm* a tie
une **matière** *nf* a (school) subject
le **matin** *nm* (in the) morning
mauvais/mauvaise *adj* bad
me (to) me
méchant/méchante *adj* bad,
naughty
une **médaille** *nf* a medal
un **médecin** *nm* a doctor (**une femme
médecin** = a woman doctor)
meilleur/meilleure *adj* better
le/la **meilleur/meilleure** *adj* the best
un **mélange** *nm* a mixture
mélanger *v* to mix
même* *adj* same, even
la **mémoire** *nf* memory
mentionner *v* to mention
la **mer** *nf* sea
Merci! Thanks!
mercredi *nm* (on) Wednesday
une **mère** *nf* a mother
merveilleux/merveilleuse *adj*
wonderful
un **métier** *nm* a job, profession
le **métro** *nm* the Underground
mettre *v* to put; to put on (*an item of
clothing*)
à **midi** at midday
mille a thousand
des **milliers de** thousands of
mince* *adj* thin, slender
à **minuit** at midnight
mis put *pp of* **mettre**
les **mitaines** *nf pl* fingerless gloves,
mittens
moche* *adj* ugly, awful
la **mode** *nf* fashion
à la **mode** fashionable
moi me (*after prepositions such
as* **après**, **chez** *etc. or
for emphasis*)
au **moins** at least (*with numbers*)
du **moins** at least
le **mois** *nm* month
mon/ma/mes my
le **monde** *nm* the world
**mondial/mondiale/mondiaux/
mondiales** *adj* world
monsieur (*pl* **messieurs**) Sir
une **montagne** *nf* a mountain
monter *v* † to go up
montrer *v* to show
un **morceau** (*pl* **des morceaux**) *nm*
a bit, piece
mort/morte *adj* dead; *pp of* **mourir**
un **mot** *nm* a word
une **moto(cyclette)** *nf* a motorbike

mourir *v* † to die
le mur *nm* wall
mûr/mûre *adj* ripe
la musculation *nf* weight training, bodybuilding
un musée *nm* a museum
un musicien *nm* a (*male*) musician
une musicienne *nf* a (*female*) musician
la musique *nf* music

nager *v* to swim
la naissance *nf* birth
naître *v* † to be born
la natation *nf* swimming
faire naufrage to be shipwrecked
ne ... jamais never
ne ... pas not
ne ... personne no one
ne ... plus no longer, not any more
ne ... rien nothing
né/née born *pp of* naître
la neige *nf* snow
il neige it's snowing
nettoyer *v* to clean
neuf nine
neuvième* *adj* ninth
le nez *nm* nose
Noël *nm* Christmas
noir/noire *adj* black
un nombre *nm* a number
non no
le nord *nm* north
notre/nos our
la nourriture *nf* food
nous we
nouveau/nouvel/nouvelle/
    nouveaux/nouvelles *adj* new
novembre *nm* November
le noyau d'olive (*pl* des noyaux) *nm*
    olive stone
un nuage *nm* a cloud
la nuit *nf* night
nul/nulle *adj* rubbish, terrible
un numéro (de téléphone) *nm*
    a (telephone) number
numéroter *v* to number

occupé/occupée *adj* 1) busy
    2) occupied
s' occuper de *v* † to look after
octobre *nm* October
un œil (*pl* les yeux) *nm* an eye
un œuf *nm* an egg
offrir *v* 1) to give (*as a present*) 2) to
offer
on we, you, one
on y va! let's go!
ils/elles ont they have − *from* avoir
onze eleven
une orange *nf* an orange
orange* *adj* orange
un ordinateur *nm* a computer
un ordinateur portable *nm* a laptop
une oreille *nf* an ear
l' orthographe *nf* spelling
ou or
où where
oublier *v* to forget
l' ouest *nm* west
oui yes
ouvert/ouverte *adj* open;
    pp of ouvrir
ouvrir *v* to open

le pain *nm* bread
la paix *nf* peace
un pantalon *nm* (a pair of) trousers
Pâques *nm pl* Easter
par through
C'est par où? How do you get there?
par contre on the other hand
par ici through here, around here
par an, mois, semaine... per year,
    per month, per week...
un parapluie *n* an umbrella
un parc d'attractions *nm* a theme park
parce que because
Pardon! Excuse me!
entre parenthèses in brackets
paresseux/paresseuse *adj* lazy
parfait/parfaite *adj* perfect
un parking *nm* a car park
parler *v* to speak
partager *v* to share
un/une partenaire *nm/nf* a partner
participer à *v* to take part in
une partie *nf* a part (*not* 'party'!)
faire partie de to be part of
partir *v* † to leave
pas not; *see* ne ... pas
Pas de problème! No problem!
un passeport *nm* a passport
passer *v* 1) to spend (*time*) 2) to
    take (*an exam*)
un passe-temps *nm* a hobby
passionnant/passionnante *adj*
    fascinating
passionner *v* to fascinate
le patinage *nm* skating
patiner *v* to skate

pauvre* *adj* poor
un pays *nm* a country
les Pays-Bas *nm pl* the Netherlands
la pêche *nf* fishing
une pêche *nf* a peach
une pelouse *nf* a lawn
pendant during, for (*time*)
penser *v* to think
perdre *v* to lose
perdu/perdue *adj* lost; *pp of* perdre
un père *nm* a father
permettre (à + *person* de +
    infinitive) *v* to allow (someone to do
    something)
permis/permise *adj* allowed; *pp of*
    permettre
une personne *nf* a person
personne *see* ne ... personne
la pétanque *nf* bowls game played in
    France
petit/petite *adj* small
petit à petit little by little
les petits-enfants *nm pl* grandchildren
un peu a little
avoir peur to be afraid
peureux/peureuse *adj* fearful, timid
je/tu peux I/you can − *from* pouvoir
une pharmacie *nf* a chemist's
une phrase *nf* a sentence
une pièce *nf* 1) a room 2) a coin
    3) (de théâtre) a play
le pied *nm* foot
à pied on foot
au pied du/de la/des at the foot of
un piercing *nm* a piercing
une pincée de a pinch of
une piscine *nf* a swimming pool
pittoresque* *adj* picturesque
une place *nf* a city/town square
une plage *nf* a beach
avec plaisir! gladly! with pleasure!
plat/plate *adj* flat (*even*)
un plat *nm* 1) a dish (*bowl etc.*)
    2) a dish (*recipe*)
plein/pleine de full of
pleurer *v* to cry
il pleut it's raining − *from* pleuvoir
pleuvoir *v* to rain
la plongée *nf* diving
la pluie *nf* rain
la plupart *nf* the majority, most
plus more
plus *see* ne ... plus
plus beau/grand/petit... more
    beautiful, bigger, smaller...

Glossaire

plus tard later
en plus in addition
plus ou moins more or less
plusieurs* *adj* several
plutôt rather
un poète *nm* a poet
le poids *nm* weight
la pointure *nf* shoe size
à pois spotted
un poisson *nm* a fish
poli/polie *adj* polite
un policier *nm* a policeman
une policière *nf* a policewoman
la politesse *nf* politeness
polluer *v* to pollute
la Pologne *nf* Poland
polonais/polonaise *adj* Polish
une pomme *nf* an apple
un portable *nm* a mobile (telephone)
portugais/portugaise *adj* Portuguese
le Portugal *nm* Portugal
poser *v* to put
poser une question *v* to ask a question
une poste *nf* a post office
un poste de police *nm* a police station
le poulet *nm* chicken
pour for
pour (+ *infinitive*) in order to...
pourquoi? why?
pourtant nevertheless
pousser *v* to push, to grow
pouvoir *v* to be able to, 'can'
pratiquer *v* to practise, to do (*e.g. a sport*)
préféré/préférée *adj* favourite
je préfère I prefer – *from* préférer
préférer *v* to prefer
premier/première *adj* first
prendre *v* to take
se préparer (+ à + *infinitive*) *v* † to prepare oneself (to do something)
près de close to
presque almost
principal/principale/principaux/principales *adj* main
pris taken *pp of* prendre
privé/privée *adj* private
Pas de problème! No problem!
prochain/prochaine *adj* next
un prof(esseur) *nm* teacher (used for both men and women)
le printemps *nm* spring (*season*)
un projet *nm* a project, plan
une promenade *nf* a walk
une promenade en bateau *nf* a boat trip
se promener *v* † to go for a walk

proposer *v* 1) to suggest 2) to offer
une prune *nf* a plum
pu been able to *pp of* pouvoir
la publicité *nf* advertising
puer *v* to stink
puis then
puisque since
un pull *nm* a pullover, jumper

se qualifier *v* † to qualify
quand? when?
quand même even so
quarante forty
quarante-deux forty-two
quarante et un forty-one
un quart d'heure *nm* a quarter of an hour
un quartier *nm* a neighbourhood
quatorze fourteen
quatre four
quatre-vingts eighty
quatre-vingt-dix ninety
quatre-vingt-onze ninety-one
quatre-vingt-un eighty-one
quatrième* *adj* fourth
que which, that, whom
Qu'est-ce que...? What...?
Qu'est-ce que c'est? What is it?
Qu'est-ce qu'il y a? What's the matter?
Que faire? What should I do?
quel/quelle/quels/quelles? which?
Quelle blague! What rubbish!
Quelle surprise! What a surprise!
quelque* *adj* some
quelque chose something
quelqu'un someone
Pas question! No way!
une queue *nf* 1) a tail 2) a queue
qui who, which, that
quinze fifteen
quinze jours a fortnight
quitter *v* to leave (*place*)
quoi? what?

raconter *v* to tell (*a story*)
raide* *adj* straight (*of hair*)
avoir raison to be right
ramener *v* to bring/take back
ranger *v* to tidy up
une raquette *nf* a racket
rasé/rasée *adj* shaved
ravi/ravie *adj* delighted
ravissant/ravissante *adj* lovely
à rayures striped

réaliste* *adj* realistic
une recette *nf* a recipe
recevoir *v* to receive, to get
reconnaître *v* to recognise
reconnu recognised *pp of* reconnaître
reçu received *pp of* recevoir
refaire *v* to redo
réfléchir *v* to think, to reflect
un refuge *nm* 1) a shelter 2) a traffic island
regarder *v* to look at, to watch
je regrette I'm sorry
remarquer *v* to notice
remercier *v* to thank
remettre de l'ordre *v* to put back in order
remplacer *v* to replace
une rencontre *nf* a meeting
rencontrer *v* to meet
rendre *v* to give back, to return (*something*)
renseigner *v* to give information
les renseignements *nm pl* information
rentrer *v* † to go home
un repas *nm* a meal
repérer *v* to spot, to find
répéter *v* to repeat
répondre *v* to reply
une réponse *nf* a reply
se reposer *v* † to rest
résister (+ à) *v* to resist
rester *v* † to stay
un resto *nm* a restaurant (*short for* un restaurant)
un résultat *nm* a result
en retard late
retourner *v* † to go back
retrouver *v* to meet
réussi/réussie *adj* successful
réussir à *v* to succeed at/in
un rêve *nm* a dream
de rêve *adj* ideal
se réveiller *v* † to wake up
revenir *v* † to come back
Au revoir! Goodbye!
rien nothing; *see* ne ... rien
De rien! You're welcome!
rigolo/rigolote *adj* funny
rire *v* to laugh
une rivière *nf* a river
le riz *nm* rice
une robe *nf* a dress
un roller *nm* a roller skate
romain/romaine *adj* Roman
rose* *adj* pink
la roue *nf* wheel
rouge* *adj* red
rougir *v* to blush

rouler *v* to move (*of a vehicle*)
la route *nf* road, route
roux/rousse *adj* auburn, ginger (*used to describe hair*)
une rue *nf* a street, road
russe* *adj* Russian
la Russie *nf* Russia

un sac *nm* a bag
un sac à main *nm* a handbag
sain/saine *adj* healthy
je sais I know – *from* **savoir**
une salle *nf* a (large) room, hall
un salon *nm* a sitting room
Salut! Hello!/Bye! (*to a friend*)
samedi *nm* (on) Saturday
sans without
sauf except
sauver *v* to save
savoir *v* to know (*a fact*), to know how to
seize sixteen
le sel *nm* salt
selon according to
une semaine *nf* a week
la semoule *nf* semolina
je sens 1) I feel 2) I smell – *from* **sentir**
sentir *v* 1) to feel 2) to smell
sept seven
septième* *adj* seventh
septembre *nm* September
un serpent *nm* a snake
un/une serveur/serveuse *nm/nf* a waiter/waitress
une serviette *nf* a napkin, serviette
servir *v* to serve
seul/seule *adj* alone
seulement only
un short *nm* (a pair of) shorts
si if
si yes (*in contradiction*)
siffler *v* 1) to whistle 2) to hiss
s'il te plaît please (*to a friend or relative*)
s'il vous plaît please (*polite form, especially to a stranger*)
six six
sixième* *adj* sixth
un slip *nm* (a pair of) pants
j'ai soif I'm thirsty
le soir *nm* (in the) evening
une soirée *nf* 1) an evening 2) a party
soixante sixty
soixante-deux sixty-two
soixante-dix seventy
soixante-douze seventy-two
soixante et onze seventy-one
soixante et un sixty-one

le soleil *nm* sun, sunshine
il fait du soleil it's sunny
nous sommes we are – *from* **être**
son/sa/ses his/her/its
un sondage *nm* a poll, survey
ils/elles sont they are – *from* **être**
une sortie *nf* 1) an exit 2) a trip out
sortir *v* † to go out
une soucoupe volante *nf* a flying saucer
souffler *v* to blow
à tes/vos souhaits! bless you!
souligné/soulignée *adj* underlined
sourire *v* to smile
un sourire *nm* a smile
une souris *nf* a mouse
un souvenir *nm* 1) a memory 2) a souvenir
sportif/sportive *adj* sporty
un sportif *nm* a sportsman
une sportive *nf* a sportswoman
un stade *nm* a stadium
une station *nf* a station (*e.g. on the Métro*)
une station spatiale *nf* a space station
un stylo *nm* a pen
su known *pp of* **savoir**
le sucre *nm* sugar
les sucreries *nf pl* sweet things
le sud *nm* south
la Suède *nf* Sweden
suédois/suédoise *adj* Swedish
je suis I am – *from* **être**
la Suisse *nf* Switzerland
suisse* *adj* Swiss
un supermarché *nm* a supermarket
sûr/sûre (+ **de**) *adj* sure (about, of)
un surnom *nm* a nickname
surveçu survived *pp of* **survivre**
survivre *v* to survive
un sweat à capuche *nm* a hooded top

un tableau (*pl* **des tableaux**) *nm* a picture
la taille *nf* size, height
tard late
te (to) you (*to a friend or well-known adult*)
tel/telle/tels/telles que such as
un téléchargement *nm* a download
le temps *nm* time, weather
de temps en temps from time to time
le temps libre *nm* free time
tenir *v* 1) to hold 2) to keep
tenu held, kept *pp of* **tenir**
la tenue *nf* outfit
terminer *v* to finish
la Terre *nf* Earth (= *planet*)
la tête *nf* head

le thé *nm* tea
le thon *nm* tuna
le tir à l'arc *nm* archery
toi you (*after prepositions such as* **après**, **chez** *etc. or for emphasis*)
un toit *nm* a roof
tomber *v* † to fall
ton/ta/tes your (*to a friend or well-known adult*)
avoir tort to be wrong
tôt early
faire le tour de to go round
une tour *nf* a tower
un tournoi *nm* a tournament
tous les jours/matins every day/morning
tout à coup suddenly
tout de suite immediately
tout droit straight on
tout le monde everyone
une traduction *nf* a translation
traduire *v* to translate
être en train de to be in the process of
une tranche *nf* a slice
le travail *nm* work
travailler *v* to work
à travers across, through
traverser *v* to cross
treize thirteen
trente thirty
trente-deux thirty-two
trente et un thirty-one
très very
le trésor *nm* treasure
trois three
troisième* *adj* third
trop too
un trou *nm* a hole, gap
une trousse *nf* a pencil case
trouver *v* to find
tu you (*to a friend or well-known adult*)
tuer *v* to kill

un a (+ *nm*)
une a (+ *nf*)
uni/unie *adj* plain (= *solid-coloured*)
unique* *adj* only
usé/usée *adj* worn (out)
user *v* to wear out
utiliser *v* to use

Glossaire

il/elle/on **va** he/she goes; we/you go
   – *from* **aller**
les **vacances** *nf pl* holidays
les **vacances scolaires** *nf pl* school
   holidays
je **vais** I go – *from* **aller**
faire la **vaisselle** to do the washing-up
une **valise** *nf* a suitcase
tu **vas** you go – *from* **aller**
vécu lived *pp of* **vivre**
un **vélo** *nm* a bike
à **vélo** by bike
un **vendeur** *nm* a salesman
une **vendeuse** *nf* a saleswoman
vendre *v* to sell
vendredi *nm* (on) Friday
venir *v* † to come
le **vent** *nm* wind
il y a du **vent** *it's* windy
le **ventre** *nm* stomach
venu came *pp of* **venir**
le **verglas** *nm* (black) ice (*on road*)
vérifier *v* to check
vers towards; around (*time*)
verser *v* to pour
vert/verte *adj* green
une **veste** *nf* a jacket (*not* 'vest'!)
les **vêtements** *nm pl* clothes
ils/elles **veulent** they want – *from* **vouloir**
il/elle/on **veut** he/she wants; we/you want
   – *from* **vouloir**
je/tu **veux** I/you want – *from* **vouloir**
la **viande** *nf* meat
la **vie** *nf* life
ils/elles **viennent** they come – *from* **venir**
je/tu **viens** I/you come – *from* **venir**
il/elle/on **vient** he/she comes, we/you come
   – *from* **venir**
vieux/vieil/vieille/vieux/vieilles
   adj old
une **ville** *nf* a town, city
le **vin** *nm* wine
vingt twenty
vingt-deux twenty-two
vingt et un twenty-one
un **violon** *nm* a violin
vite* *adj* fast
vivant/vivante *adj* living
vivre *v* to live
voici here is/here are
voilà there is/there are
la **voile** *nf* sailing
voir *v* to see
un **voisin** *nm* a (*male*) neighbour
une **voisine** *nf* a (*female*) neighbour

une **voiture** *nf* a car
une **voix** *nf* a voice
le **vol** *nm* 1) flight 2) theft
voler *v* 1) to fly 2) to steal
un **voleur** *nm* a (*male*) thief
une **voleuse** *nf* a (*female*) thief
votre/vos your
je **voudrais** I would like – *from* **vouloir**
vouloir *v* to want
vous (to) you (*plural or polite*)
un **voyage** *nm* a journey
Bon **voyage!** Have a good trip!
voyager *v* to travel
vrai/vraie true
vraiment really
vu seen *pp of* **voir**
la **vue** *nf* view

Y

y there
y compris including
un **yaourt** *nm* a yoghurt
les **yeux** *nm pl* eyes – *see* **un œil**

Glossary

to be **able to** pouvoir *v*
about (= *approximately*) à peu près,
environ; (*with clock times*) vers
after après
(in the) **afternoon** l'après-midi *nm*
(a week) **ago** il y a (une semaine)
almost presque
also aussi
always toujours
I **am...** je suis...
I **am 14 years old** j'ai quatorze ans
April avril *nm*
arm le bras *nm*
as comme
to **ask** demander *v*
to be **asleep** dormir *v*
at Robert's (house) chez Robert
athletics l'athlétisme *nm*
August août *nm*
autumn l'automne *nm*

bad mauvais/mauvaise *adj*
a **bag** un sac *nm*
a **baker's (shop)** une boulangerie *nf*
a **bank** une banque *nf*
to have a **bath** prendre *v* un bain
to **be** être *v*
beautiful beau/bel/belle/beaux/
belles *adj*
because parce que
to go to **bed** se coucher *v* †
before avant
behind derrière
to **believe** croire *v*
the **best** le meilleur/la meilleure
between entre
big grand/grande *adj*
a **bike** un vélo *nm*
a **birthday** un anniversaire *nm*
black noir/noire *adj*
blonde blond/blonde *adj*
a **blouse** un chemisier *nm*
blue bleu/bleue *adj*
a **boat** un bateau *nm* (*pl* les bateaux)
body le corps *nm*
a **book** un livre *nm*
a **bookshop** une librairie *nf*
boring ennuyeux/ennuyeuse *adj*
a **bottle** une bouteille *nf*
a **bowl** un bol *nm*
bread le pain *nm*
to **break** casser *v*
breakfast le petit déjeuner *nm*
British britannique* *adj*
the **British** les Britanniques *nm pl*

broken cassé/cassée *adj*
brother le frère *nm*
brown brun/brune *adj*; (*of eyes*)
marron* *adj*
to **brush one's teeth** se brosser les
dents *v* †
a **bus** un (auto)bus *nm*
busy occupé/occupée *adj*
but mais
a **butcher's (shop)** une boucherie *nf*
butter le beurre *nm*
to **buy** acheter *v*

a **cake** un gâteau *nm* (*pl* les gâteaux)
can *see* **able to**
a **car** une voiture *nf*
to go by **car** aller *v* en voiture
a **car park** un parking *nm*
a (TV) **channel** une chaîne *nf*
cheap bon marché* *adj*
a **chemist's (shop)** une pharmacie *nf*
chips les frites *nf pl*
Christmas Noël *nm*
Happy **Christmas!** Joyeux Noël!
a **church** une église *nf*
a **cinema** un cinéma *nm*
a **city** une grande ville *nf*
the **city centre** le centre-ville *nm*
close to près de
clothes les vêtements *nm pl*
a **coach** (*transport*) un car *nm*
a **coat** un manteau *nm* (*pl* les
manteaux)
I'm **cold** j'ai froid
it's **cold** il fait froid
to **come** venir *v* †
a **computer** un ordinateur *nm*
a **country** un pays *nm*
in the **country(side)** à la campagne
cousin le cousin *nm* / la cousine *nf*
crisps les chips *nf pl*
to **cross** traverser *v*
to **cry** pleurer *v*
a **cup** une tasse *nf*
curly frisé/frisée *adj*
to go **cycling** faire *v* du vélo

daughter la fille *nf*
a **day** un jour *nm*, une journée *nf*
December décembre *nm*
to **describe** décrire *v*
a **desk** (*in office*) un bureau *nm*;
despite malgré
a **dictionary** un dictionnaire *nm*
to have **dinner** dîner *v*

to **discuss** discuter *v*
diving la plongée *nf*
to **download** télécharger *v*
downstairs en bas
to **draw** dessiner *v*
a **dress** une robe *nf*
to get **dressed** s'habiller *v* †
a **drink** une boisson *nf*
to **drink** boire *v*

each chaque*
an **ear** une oreille *nf*
early de bonne heure
Happy **Easter!** Joyeuses Pâques!
to **eat** manger *v*
an **egg** un œuf *nm*
eight huit
eighteen dix-huit
eighty quatre-vingts
to **enjoy oneself** s'amuser *v* †
to **enter** entrer *v* †
even même
(in the) **evening** le soir *nm*
everybody/everyone tout le monde
everything tout
except sauf
Excuse me! Excusez-moi!, Pardon!
an **exercise book** un cahier *nm*
expensive cher/chère *adj*
to **explain** expliquer *v*
an **eye** un œil *nm* (*pl* les yeux)

face le visage *nm*
to **fall asleep** s'endormir *v* †
family la famille *nf*
a **fan** un/une fan *nm/nf*, (*sports*) un
supporter *nm*
fashion(able) (à) la mode *nf*
a **fast-food restaurant** un fast-food *nm*
fat gros/grosse *adj*
father le père *nm*
favourite préféré/préférée *adj*
February février *nm*
fifteen quinze
fifty cinquante
I'm **fine!** Ça va!
a **finger** un doigt *nm*
to **finish** finir *v*, terminer *v*
the **first** le premier *nm* / la première *nf*
at **first** d'abord
fish le poisson *nm*
a **fish shop** une poissonnerie *nf*
fit en forme

Glossary

five cinq
food la nourriture *nf*
a foot un pied *nm*
to go on foot aller *v* à pied
football le foot(ball) *nm*
for pour; (*time past*) pendant; (*future time*) pour
forbidden interdit/interdite *adj*
to forget oublier *v*
a fork une fourchette *nf*
a fortnight une quinzaine *nf*, quinze jours
forty quarante
four quatre
fourteen quatorze
France la France *nf*
free (*without cost*) gratuit/gratuite *adj*; (*liberated*) libre* *adj*
French français/française *adj*
the French les Français *nm pl*
in French en français
a Frenchman un Français *nm*
a Frenchwoman une Française *nf*
(on) Friday vendredi *nm*
a friend (*male*) un ami, un copain *nm*; (*female*) une amie, une copine *nf*
friendly amical/amicale *adj*
friendship l'amitié *nf*
fruit les fruits *nm pl*
full (of) plein/pleine *adj* (de)
to have fun s'amuser *v* †

a garden un jardin *nm*
generally en général
to get (= *to receive*) recevoir *v*
to get dressed s'habiller *v* †
to get off descendre *v* † (de)
to get on to monter *v* † (dans)
to get on with s'entendre avec *v* †
to get up se lever *v* †
ginger (-haired) roux/rousse *adj*
to give donner *v*; (*as a present*) offrir *v*
a glass un verre *nm*
glasses les lunettes *nf pl*
to go aller *v* †
to go down descendre *v* †
to go for a walk se promener *v* †
to go home rentrer *v* †
to go in entrer *v* †
to go out sortir *v* †
to go to bed se coucher *v* †
to go to sleep s'endormir *v* †
to go up monter *v* †
to go up to the top (of the tower) monter *v* † au sommet (de la tour)
good bon/bonne *adj*
Goodbye! Au revoir!; Salut!

grandchildren les petits-enfants *nm pl*
grandfather le grand-père *nm*
grandmother la grand-mère *nf*
grandparents les grands-parents *nm pl*
It's great! C'est genial! C'est super!
Great Britain la Grande-Bretagne *nf*
green vert/verte *adj*
grey gris/grise *adj*
a grocer's (shop) une épicerie *nf*
to guess deviner *v*

hair les cheveux *nm pl*
a hairdresser's un salon de coiffure *nm*
a half-hour une demi-heure *nf*
ham le jambon *nm*
hand la main *nf*
handsome beau/bel/belle/beaux/ belles *adj*
happy heureux(euse), content(e) *adj*
Happy birthday! Bon anniversaire!
hard dur/dure *adj*, difficile* *adj*
a hat un chapeau *nm* (*pl* les chapeaux)
to hate détester *v*
to have avoir *v*
to have to devoir *v*
he il
a head teacher un(e) directeur(trice) *nm/nf*
to have a headache, avoir *v* mal à la tête, au ventre...
healthy sain/saine *adj*
Hello! Bonjour!; (*in the evening*) Bonsoir!; (*to a friend any time*) Salut!; (*on the telephone*) Allô!
her (= *object of sentence*) la; (= *belonging to*) son/sa/ses
to her lui
here is/here are... voici...
to hide cacher *v*
him le
to him lui
his son/sa/ses
history l'histoire *nf*
to hit frapper *v*
hobbies les passe-temps *nm pl*
holidays les vacances *nf pl*
on holiday en vacances
at home à la maison; chez moi, toi, lui...
homework les devoirs *nm pl*
to hope espérer *v*
a hospital un hôpital *nm*
I'm hot j'ai chaud
it's hot il fait chaud
a house une maison *nf*
How do you pronounce it? Ça se prononce comment?

How do you write/spell it? Ça s'écrit comment?
How much is it? Ça fait combien?
How old are you? Tu as quel âge?/ Vous avez quel âge?
a hundred cent
I'm hungry j'ai faim
in a hurry pressé/pressée *adj*

I je
an ice cream une glace *nf*
ill malade* *adj*
immediately tout de suite
in (*e.g. a bag*) dans
in France en France
in January... en janvier...
in the country à la campagne
in the suburbs en banlieue
in town en ville
an inhabitant un(e) habitant(e) *nm/nf*
interesting intéressant(e) *adj*
Internet l'Internet *nm*
Is there...? Il y a...?
it (*nm*) il; (*nf*) elle
its son/sa/ses
It's seven o'clock Il est sept heures

January janvier *nm*
(a pair of) jeans un jean *nm*
jewellery les bijoux *nm pl*
a job un boulot *nm*
to go jogging faire *v* du footing/jogging *nm*
a journey un voyage *nm*
July juillet *nm*
June juin *nm*

a knee un genou *nm* (*pl* les genoux)
a knife un couteau *nm* (*pl* les couteaux)
to know (*a person, place*) connaître *v*; (*a fact*) savoir *v*

a language une langue *nf*
a laptop un ordinateur portable *nm*
last dernier/dernière *adj*
last week la semaine dernière
to be late être *v* en retard
to laugh rire *v*
to learn apprendre *v*
at least du moins; (*numbers*) au moins
to leave partir *v* †; (*a place, person, job*) quitter *v*

to/on the left à gauche
leg la jambe *nf*
a lesson un cours *nm*, une leçon *nf*
a library une bibliothèque *nf*
life la vie *nf*
to like aimer *v*
I like j'aime
I like him je l'aime bien)
I like it je l'aime, ça me plaît
I don't like... je déteste...
I would like... je voudrais...
to listen to écouter *v*
to live vivre *v*; (*in a place*) habiter *v*
I live (in London) j'habite à Londres
long long/longue *adj*
to look regarder *v*
to lose perdre *v*
lots of beaucoup de
love l'amour *nm*
to love aimer *v adorer v*
I love... j'adore...
loyal fidèle* *adj*
luggage les bagages *nm pl*
lunch le déjeuner *nm*
to have lunch déjeuner *v*

to make faire *v*
make-up le maquillage *nm*
March mars *nm*
a market un marché *nm*
It doesn't matter! Ça ne fait rien!
May mai *nm*
(to) me me
a meal un repas *nm*
meat la viande *nf*
to meet rencontrer *v*; **se** retrouver *v* †
a memory un souvenir *nm*
at midday à midi
at midnight à minuit
milk le lait *nm*
I don't mind! Cela m'est égal!
a mobile (telephone) un portable *nm*
(on) Monday lundi *nm*
money l'argent *nm*
a month un mois *nm*
for months pendant quelques mois
more (than) plus que
in the morning le matin *nm*
mother la mère *nf*
a motorbike une moto(cyclette) *nf*
a mouth une bouche *nf*
an MP3 player un baladeur MP3 *nm*
a museum un musée *nm*
music la musique *nf*
a musician un(e) musicien(ne) *nm/nf*
I must je dois
my mon/ma/mes
at my house chez moi

I need... J'ai besoin de...
neighbourhood le quartier *nm*
never ne ... jamais
new nouveau/nouvel/nouvelle/
nouveaux/nouvelles *adj*
a newspaper un journal *nm* (*pl* les
journaux)
next to à côté du/de la/des
nice gentil/gentille *adj*, sympa* *adj*
night la nuit *nf*
nine neuf
nineteen dix-neuf
nose le nez *nm*
not ne ... pas *e.g.* Je n'aime <u>pas</u> le
fromage (= *I don't like cheese*)
to notice remarquer *v*
November novembre *nm*
a number (*quantity*) un nombre *nm*;
(*digit*) un chiffre *nm*; (*telephone*)
un numéro *nm*

October octobre *nm*
of course bien sûr
an office un bureau *nm*
often souvent
OK! D'accord!
old vieux/vieil/vieille/vieux/vieilles *adj*
on sur
only seulement
open ouvert/ouverte *adj*
in your opinion à ton/votre avis
opposite en face du/de la/des
an orange une orange *nf*
orange orange* *adj*
in order to pour (+ *infinitive*)
our notre/nos

my parents mes parents *nm pl*
a park un parc *nm*, un jardin public *nm*
a party une fête *nf*, une boum *nf*
to pay payer *v*
a pen un stylo *nm*
a pencil un crayon *nm*
a pencil case une trousse *nf*
people les gens *nm pl*
pink rose* *adj*
a plate une assiette *nf*
to play (sport) jouer *v* au/à la/aux
to play (muscial instrument) jouer *v*
du/de la

Please! (*to a friend or relative*) S'il te
plaît!; (*to more than one person, or
to someone you don't know well*) S'il
vous plaît!
a police station un poste de police *nm*
polite poli/polie *adj*
a post office une poste *nf*
a present un cadeau *nm* (*pl les
cadeaux*)
a (TV) programme une émission *nf*
a pupil un élève *nm* / une élève *nf*
to put mettre *v*

a quarter of an hour un quart
d'heure *nm*
It's a quarter past seven Il est sept
heures et quart
It's a quarter to seven Il est sept
heures moins le quart
quick vite* *adj*
quiet calme* *adj*; tranquille* *adj*
quite assez

a railway station une gare *nf*
it's raining il pleut
really vraiment
to receive recevoir *v*
to read lire *v*
red rouge* *adj*
to refuse refuser *v*
to reply répondre *v*
to rest se reposer *v* †
she's right elle a raison
to/on the right à droite
a room une pièce *nf*
It's rubbish! C'est nul!
to run courir *v*

sad triste* *adj*
to go sailing faire *v* de la voile
(on) Saturday samedi *nm*
to say dire *v*
See you later! À tout à l'heure!
See you soon! À bientôt!
to sell vendre *v*
to send envoyer *v*
September septembre *nm*
seven sept
seventeen dix-sept

Glossary

several plusieurs* *adj*
(That's a) shame! Dommage!
a shirt une chemise *nf*
a shoe une chaussure *nf*
a shop un magasin *nm*; (*small*) une boutique *nf*
to go shopping faire *v* du shopping
short court/courte *adj*
(a pair of) shorts un short *nm*
to have a shower se doucher *v* †
to sing chanter *v*
sister la sœur *nf*
six six
sixteen seize
sixty soixante
size la taille *nf*, (*shoe*) la pointure *nf*
to go skateboarding faire *v* du skate
a skirt une jupe *nf*
slim mince* *adj*
slow lent/lente *adj*
small petit/petite *adj*
to smile sourire *v*
it's snowing il neige
so si
a sock une chaussette *nf*
a song une chanson *nf*
some du/de la/des
someone quelqu'un
something quelque chose
sometimes quelquefois
son le fils *nm*
soon bientôt
sorry désolé/désolée *adj*
to speak parler *v*
to spend (*money*) dépenser *v*; (*time*) passer *v*
a spoon une cuiller *nf*
a sportsman / sportswoman un sportif *nm* / une sportive *nf*
spring (*season*) le printemps *nm*
to stay rester *v* †
stomach le ventre *nm*
a story une histoire *nf*
straight on (tout) droit
a street une rue *nf*
to study étudier *v*
my stuff (*things*) mes affaires *nf pl*
suburbs la banlieue *nf*
in the suburbs en banlieue
suddenly tout à coup
summer l'été *nm*
the sun le soleil *nm*
(on) Sunday dimanche *nm*
a supermarket un supermarché *nm*
to go surfing faire *v* du surf
sweet doux/douce *adj*
to go swimming faire *v* de la natation
a swimming pool une piscine *nf*

to take prendre *v*
tall grand/grande *adj*
a teacher un professeur *nm*
a team une équipe *nf*
teeth les dents *nm pl*
to telephone téléphoner à *v*
a television programme une émission *nf*
to tell dire *v*; (*a story*) raconter *v*
ten dix
Thank you! Merci!
the (*nm*) le; (*nf*) la; (*pl*) les
their leur/leurs
them les
to them leur
there y – e.g. j'y suis allé (= *I went there*); (= *over there*) là
there is/are... il y a...
there isn't/aren't any... il n'y a pas de...
they (*nm*) ils; (*nf*) elles
thin (*skinny*) maigre* *adj*; (*slender*) mince* *adj*
a thing une chose *nf*
I'm thirsty j'ai soif
thirteen treize
thirty trente
this (*nm*) ce/cet; (*nf*) cette; (*pl*) ces
thousand mille
three trois
throat la gorge *nf*
to throw jeter *v*
(on) Thursday jeudi *nm*
a ticket un billet *nm*
What time is it? Quelle heure est-il?
today aujourd'hui
tomorrow demain
too (much) trop
towards vers
a town centre un centre-ville *nm*
in town en ville
to go by train prendre *v* le train
to train s'entraîner *v* †
trainers les baskets *nf pl*
to travel voyager *v*
(a pair of) trousers un pantalon *nm*
to try essayer *v*
(on) Tuesday mardi *nm*
twelve douze
twenty vingt
two deux

ugly laid/laide *adj*, moche* *adj*
to take the Underground prendre *v* le métro
to understand comprendre *v*

unfortunately malheureusement
upstairs à l'étage, en haut
(to) us nous
usually d'habitude

vegetables les légumes *nm pl*
very très
a video game un jeu vidéo *nm* (*pl* les jeux vidéo)
voice la voix *nf*

to wait attendre *v*
to wake up se réveiller *v* †
to want vouloir *v*; avoir *v* envie de
to get washed se laver *v* †
to watch regarder *v*
water l'eau *nf*
we nous
What's the weather like? Quel temps fait-il?
(on) Wednesday mercredi *nm*
week une semaine *nf*
this weekend ce week-end *nm*
at weekends le week-end
to do weight training faire *v* de la musculation
well bien
What did you do? Qu'est-ce que tu as fait? / Qu'est-ce que vous avez fait?
What's that? Qu'est-ce que c'est que ça?
when? quand?
where? où
Where do you live? Tu habites où? / Vous habitez où?
which? quel/quelle/quels/quelles?
white blanc/blanche *adj*
to win gagner *v*
winter l'hiver *nm*
with avec
without sans
to work travailler *v*
the world le monde *nm*
to write écrire *v*
you're wrong tu as tort / vous avez tort

[Y]

a year un an *nm*, une année *nf*
yellow jaune* *adj*
yesterday hier
you (*to a friend or a relative*) tu; (*to a stranger or an adult*) vous
young jeune* *adj*
your ton/ta/tes; votre/vos